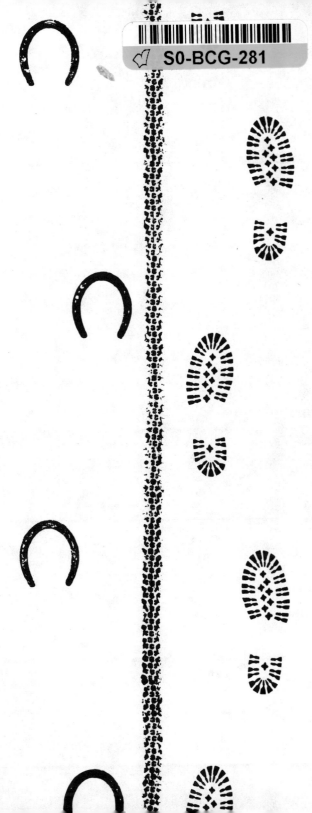

The Santa Cruz Mountains Trail Book
by Tom Taber

Seventh Edition

The parks and trails of the mountains of San Mateo, Santa Clara, and Santa Cruz Counties.

Plus...

A coastal access guide to San Mateo and Santa Cruz Counties.

The Oak Valley Press

ISBN 0-9609170-5-5

Copyright ©1994 by Tom Taber

First Edition 1976
Second Edition 1979
Third Edition 1982
Fourth Edition 1985
Fifth Edition 1988
Sixth Edition 1991

PHOTO CREDITS:
Page 94: U.S. Geological Survey.
All other photos by Tom Taber.

Front cover photo: Berry Creek Falls at Big Basin Redwoods State Park.

THE OAK VALLEY PRESS
228 Virginia Ave.,
San Mateo, CA 94402

Table of Contents

SPECIAL SECTIONS:

Introduction

The Santa Cruz Mountains are unique among all of California's coastal ranges. They are the only one of these ranges to diverge from the mainland of North America, separated partly by San Francisco Bay.

Urban development in San Francisco, southward on the Peninsula, and in the Santa Clara Valley has accentuated this separation, making the Santa Cruz Mountains an ecological island. Surrounded by the Pacific Ocean to the west, cities and the bay to the north and east, and an agricultural valley along the Pajaro River to the south, much of the native wildlife is now confined to this small range of mountains which is only about 80 miles long.

Situated on the coast midway between Mexico and Oregon, the Santa Cruz Mountains have characteristics of nearly all parts of the Coast Range. Giant redwoods in moist, foggy valleys are reminiscent of Humboldt County far to the north. Chaparral on dry, sun-baked ridges seem typical of Santa Barbara County to the south. Grasslands and oak woodlands are reminders of the inner coast ranges away from the marine influence to the east. The Santa Cruz Mountains also have rocky and sandy seacoasts,

Grassland

Riperian

Oakwood

Coastal Scrub

wetlands, coastal scrub, Douglas fir forests, cypress groves, and even a few naturally occurring stands of ponderosa pine, making this small range one of the most ecologically diverse places in California.

The westward-flowing moist airmass delivers annual average precipitation exceeding 55 inches in some places on the western, seaward, side of the range (not counting considerable moisture from fog drip) and leaves the foothills inland to the east with as little as 15 inches of rain.

These varied conditions are so dramatic that in many parks and preserves in this book you will experience at least 3 or 4 ecological communities in a single short outing.

Redwood

Chaparral

Douglas Fir

Wetland

Rocky Coast

Sandy Beach

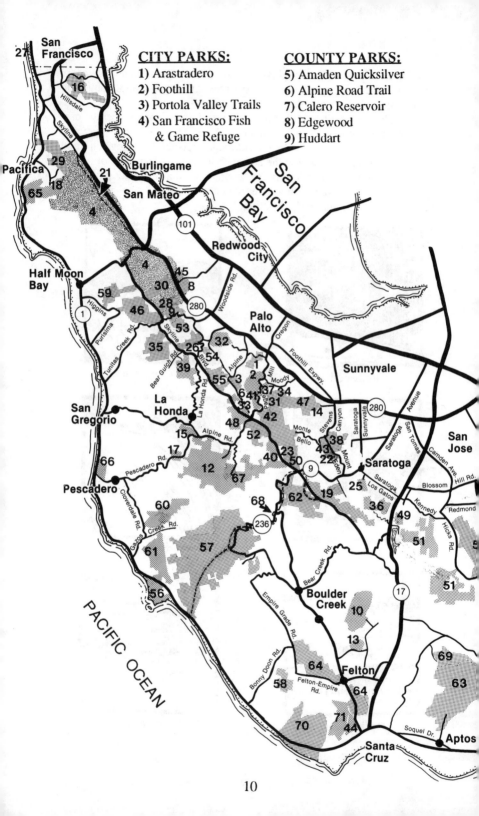

CITY PARKS:
1) Arastradero
2) Foothill
3) Portola Valley Trails
4) San Francisco Fish
   & Game Refuge

COUNTY PARKS:
5) Amaden Quicksilver
6) Alpine Road Trail
7) Calero Reservoir
8) Edgewood
9) Huddart

10) Loch Lomond
11) Mount Madonna
12) Pescadero Creek
13) Quail Hollow Ranch
14) Rancho San Antonio
15) Sam McDonald
16) San Bruno Mountain
17) San Mateo Memorial
18) San Pedro Valley
19) Sanborn Skyline
20) Santa Teresa
21) Sawyer Camp Trail
22) Stevens Creek
23) Upper Stevens Creek
24) Uvas Canyon
25) Villa Montalvo
26) Wunderlich

GOLDEN GATE NTL RECREATION AREA:
27) Fort Funston
28) Phleger Estate
29) Sweeney Ridge

PRIVATE:
30) Filoli
31) Hidden Villa Ranch
32) Jasper Ridge

OPEN SPACE:
33) Coal Creek
34) Duveneck Windmill
35) El Corte De Madera
36) El Sereno
37) Foothills
38) Fremont Older
39) La Honda Creek
40) Long Ridge
41) Los Trancos
42) Monte Bello
43) Picchetti Ranch
44) Pogonip
45) Pulgas Ridge
46) Purisima Creek
47) Rancho San Antonio
48) Russian Ridge
49) St. Joseph's Hill
50) Saratoga Gap
51) Sierra Azul
52) Skyline Ridge
53) Teague Hill
54) Thornewood
55) Windy Hill

STATE PARKS:
56) Ano Nuevo
57) Big Basin Redwoods
58) Bonny Doon
59) Burleigh Murray
60) Butano
61) Cascade Ranch
62) Castle Rock
63) Forest of Nisene Marks
64) Henry Cowell
65) McNee Ranch
66) Pescadero Marsh
67) Portola
68) Skyline-to-the-Sea Trail
69) Soquel Demonstration Forest
70) Wilder Ranch

UNIVERSITY OF CALIFORNIA:
71) Santa Cruz campus

A great slow-motion collision is happening between the North American and Pacific continental plates. The Santa Cruz Mountains, and the rest of California's Coast Ranges, are being formed by this impact.

The characteristic northwest-tending parallel ridges are shaped by the crumpling of the earth under the strain of this geologic force.

The Santa Cruz Mountains extend for about 80 miles from San Bruno Mountain, just south of San Francisco, to the Pajaro River. The range is narrowest and lowest on the northern San Francisco peninsula, getting higher, wider, and wilder to the south.

Almaden Quicksilver County Park

TO GET THERE... take Almaden Expressway south to the town of New Almaden. The Mine Hill Trail begins at the dirt road off to the west just north of Alamitos Creek. Or you can take Almaden Expressway south from San Jose, turn west on Camden and south on McAbee to the end of the road.

This 3600-acre park in the dry eastern foothills of the Santa Cruz Mountains, is well-known for its colorful mercury mining history and for its extraordinary display of spring wildflowers.

Despite many years of mining and settlement, much of this land still feels wild. For safety reasons some of the mining sites are closed to the public.

From the Almaden Road entrance, take the Mine Hill Trail uphill for sweeping views as you climb to an altitude exceeding 1,500 feet and then loop back via the Randal Mine Trail. This is an all-day hike with some strenuous grades and passes through grasslands, chaparral, and oak woodlands. From the McAbee Road entrance combine the Mine Hill and Guadalupe trails for an easy hike that loops over a ridge and past Guadalupe Reservoir.

From the McAbee Road trailhead you can walk an easy and scenic 7-mile loop by combining the Mine Hill and Guadalupe trails. Remnants of the quicksilver (mercury) mining that was the base of the local economy are seen.

The discovery of quicksilver here in 1845 by Mexican cavalry captain Andres Castillero soon resulted in the development of one of the world's greatest mercury mines. The boom went bust in the early twentieth century as the ore was exhausted and the Quicksilver Mining Company declared bankruptcy in 1912. Quicksilver, or mercury, has many uses, including the processing of gold ore. It is derived from a red rock called cinnabar.

The New Almaden Quicksilver County Park Assocation is a non-profit corporation which offers guided interpretive tours, sponsors an annual Pioneer Day, and operates the New Almaden Mining Museum on Almaden Road. For more information, call (408) 268-1729; P.O. Box 124, New Almaden, CA 95042.

Situated on the dry east side of the range, the park is covered mostly with oak woods and grasslands, which change from golden brown in summer and autumn to green in the winter and spring. The elevation ranges from less than 400 feet to more than 1,600 feet.

This park, only 11 miles south of San Jose, is open from 8 a.m. until sundown. For more information, call the Santa Clara County Parks and Recreation Department at (408) 358-3751.

Bicycle Access:
Bicycles are not permitted.

Equestrian Access:
Horses are allowed on all trails.

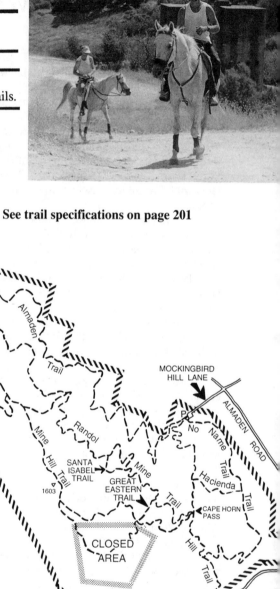

See trail specifications on page 201

Senator Mine Trail

McABEE ROAD

P

Guadalupe Trail

Mine Hill Trail

Guadalupe Trail

HICKS ROAD

Guadalupe Reservoir

New Almaden Trail

Providencia Trail

MOCKINGBIRD HILL LANE

ALMADEN ROAD

P

No Name Trail

Mine Hill Trail

Randol

Hacienda Trail

SANTA ISABEL TRAIL

GREAT EASTERN TRAIL

Mine Trail

1603

CAPE HORN PASS

CLOSED AREA

Hill Trail

P

Entrance

1 mile

Almaden Reservoir

14

Alpine Road Trail

TO GET THERE... From Highway 280 take Alpine Road about 3 miles south and west to a metal gate where it becomes a trail.

Where the pavement ends at the southwestern end of Alpine Road you can continue uphill on foot, horse, or bicycle for 2.5 miles to where it intersects Page Mill Road.

This dirt road trail gently ascends 1,000 feet through a forest of oak, bay, maple, and madrone, paralleling Corte Madera Creek which flows through the fracture zone of the San Andreas Fault.

For a more extended outing you can take connecting trails through adjacent Coal Creek Open Space Preserve and from there on to Russian Ridge and Skyline Ridge Open Space Preserves.

This road, built in 1894, is particularly popular with mountain bikers.

Near the downhill trail entrance gate you can find thin veins of coal in the roadcut on Alpine Road. This explains the the local place names "Coal Mine Ridge" and "Coal Creek".

Bicycle Access:
Bicycles are allowed.

Equestrian Access:
Horses are allowed.

Ano Nuevo State Reserve

TO GET THERE . . . The park is west of Highway I about 19 miles north of Santa Cruz.

PLEASE NOTE: To protect wildlife, access to the Wildlife Protection Area may be restricted at any time of year.

Ano Nuevo is truly one of America's great marine wildlife preserves.

Cormorants nest on ocean cliffs, tidepools abound with intertidal life, sea lions and harbor seals are commonly seen and heard on the beaches and rocks here, and even sea otters are sighted more often every year. The reserve is most popular, however, from December through April when a colony of elephant seals visits the island and peninsula for mating and bearing young. To protect these enormous mammals, and the people who come to see them, the wildlife protection area of the reserve is open only through naturalist guided walks this time of year.

Male elephant seals arrive in November to establish a breeding hierarchy and are followed in December by the females who join the harems of the dominant males. Male seals are enormous, reaching lengths of 16 feet and weighing 3 tons. Females are much smaller, at 1,200 to 2,000 pounds. Slaughtered for their oil-rich blubber, by 1892 less than 100 remained. In the 1920s the Mexican and United States governments gave them legal protection, allowing their numbers to rapidly increase since then. They first returned to Ano Nuevo Island in 1955 and are now also breeding on the peninsula. These animals, the largest members of the seal family, seem awkward on land, but they are excellent swimmers, able to dive as deep as 5,000 feet to feed mainly on rays, squids, skates, and fish.

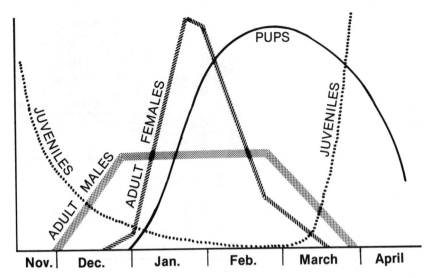

| Nov. | Dec. | Jan. | Feb. | March | April |

This chart shows the relative abundance of elephant seals during the breeding and pupping season.

This fascinating peninsula is worth exploring all year; and in fact, can be most enjoyable when most of the elephant seals and their hordes of loyal admirers are gone, and walking may be done without ranger escort. Ano Nuevo is one of the few places on the San Mateo County coast where it is possible to do some real hiking west from Highway 1.

Follow the trail west from the parking lot, passing coastal scrub, a beautiful springtime display of wildflowers, and a small marshy pond. Continue over the dunes and along the beach to the end of the peninsula, which is just over a mile from the parking lot, depending on your route.

Half a mile off the peninsula is 12-acre Ano Nuevo Island, breeding ground for elephant seals, steller sea lions, and harbor seals, and a nesting place for western gulls, pigeon guillemots, and black oystercatchers. Because of its importance to coastal wildlife, public access to the island is prohibited. This cherty shale island was part of the mainland until relatively recently in geologic time, when it was separated by wave erosion and by the gradual rising of the sea level when the ice age glaciers melted over the last ten thousand years.

This area was uplifted from the sea a mere 70-100 thousand years ago - practically yesterday to geologists - creating treacherous rocky obstacles for ships. Several major shipwrecks resulted in the construction of a lighthouse on the island in 1890. Difficult to maintain, the storm-battered station was replaced by an automated signal buoy south of the island in 1948. Today, the weathered lightkeepers' house still stands clearly visible from the mainland, now inhabited only by seals, sea lions, and birds.

A little less than a mile west of the parking lot you will pass an interpretive exhibit shelter that marks the trailhead into the Ano Nuevo

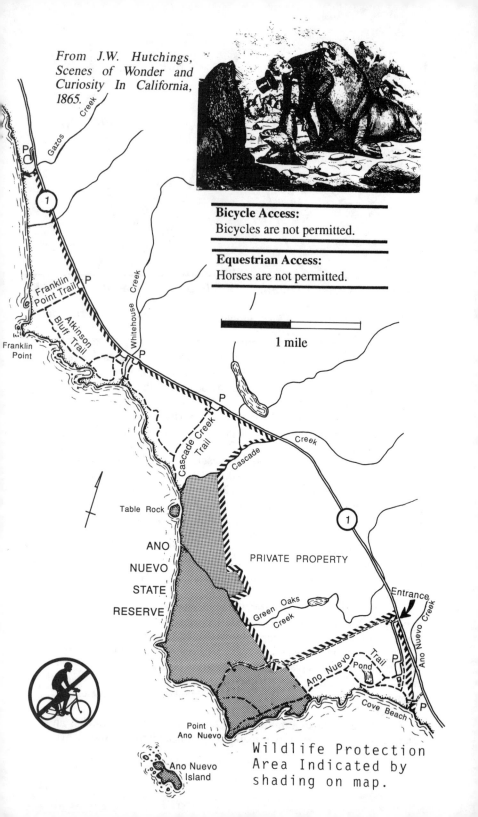

From J.W. Hutchings, *Scenes of Wonder and Curiosity In California, 1865.*

Gazos Creek

1

Franklin Point Trail

Atkinson Bluff Trail

P

Whitehouse Creek

Bicycle Access:
Bicycles are not permitted.

Equestrian Access:
Horses are not permitted.

1 mile

Franklin Point

P

P

Cascade Creek Trail

Cascade Creek

P

1

Table Rock

ANO

NUEVO

STATE

RESERVE

PRIVATE PROPERTY

Green Oaks Creek

Entrance

Ano Nuevo Creek

Ano Nuevo Trail

Pond

P

Point Ano Nuevo

Cove Beach

P

Ano Nuevo Island

Wildlife Protection Area Indicated by shading on map.

Point Wildlife Protection Area. Entry into this area between April and November is by a permit system. Park naturalists are often on hand at designated wildlife viewpoints to answer questions. Access to the intertidal zone near Ano Nuevo Point is sometimes restricted to allow increasing seal use of the beaches without disturbance.

North of Cascade Creek, the reserve can be explored all year without a permit from parking areas on the west side of Highway 1.

Tidepools exposed near the tip of the peninsula have an extraordinary abundance of marine life. Sea stars, hermit crabs, chitons, anemonies, sea urchins and many other intertidal life forms are common; and at low tide you may see what appears to be spherical boulders several feet in diameter fastened to these tidepool rocks. Closer inspection will reveal that these objects, covered with countless tiny holes, are actually tube masses, created by calciferous tube worms. Nourished largely by sea lion and seal wastes, the waters of Ano Nuevo have some of the world's largest tube worm formations. Each calcium carbonate tube mass is a community of worms and a vast network of tubal tunnels.

Harbor seals are often seen lounging on the rocks offshore, and are seen bobbing their heads above water near the shore to examine humans. Their short, plump, spotted bodies are easily identified. They mate on the island in April and May.

Humans have been visiting this area for thousands of years, as evidenced by shell mounds left by a once large Ohlone Indian habitation. For many centuries Indians lived a relatively easy life, thriving on the coast's abundance of seafood, game, acorns, and other wild edibles, and had no need for agriculture. Their discarded seashells form numerous shell mounds on this peninsula. The Indians lived in lodges usually made of willow branches arranged in 6-foot circles, bent and tied at the top, and thatched and sealed with mud. It is illegal to disturb these mounds.

Ano Nuevo has one of the oldest place names in the country, named "La Punta Del Ano Nuevo" (The Point Of The New Year) by the Spanish explorer Sebastian Vizcaino on January 3, 1603. Ano Nuevo Bay was used for shipping redwood timber from the Santa Cruz Mountains between 1853 and 1920, and the peninsula and vicinity was part of a cattle ranch established by Isaac Steele. The residence south of the parking lot was built in 1870 for Isaac's daughter, Flora Dickerman Steele. Just north are other restored ranch buildings which now house a visitors' center.

Park rangers and volunteers conduct walks in the reserve when elephant seals are here in their greatest numbers between December 15 and March 31. As of this writing, reservations are available by calling Mistix at 1(800)444 7275. Because of the popularity of these walks, be sure to make your reservations early; as much as 8 weeks in advance. For more information, call the state park office at (415)879 0227 or (415)879 2025.

Arastradero Preserve

TO GET THERE. . . From Highway 280 take Page Mill Road south and turn right on Arastradero Road to the preserve parking lot on the right side of the road.

The city of Palo Alto owns this gentle 600 acres of grassy foothills landscape. The 6 miles of trails are relatively level—ideal for small children and relaxed saunters.

Be aware that you will find little refreshing shade during hot weather, though stately old white oaks seem to be scattered conveniently for the benefit of weary travelers.

Offroad bicycles are allowed in the preserve, but not on the Perimeter Trail, which is popular with equestrians. Dogs are permitted Monday through Friday only and must be leashed and restrained at all times .

Arastradero Lake is a small reservoir just over half a mile from the parking lot by way of the Corte Madera Trail. It's a good place to pause and watch ducks, coots, and redwing blackbirds. Boats and swimming are not allowed.

For a moderate 4 mile loop around the preserve, combine the Corte Madera Trail, the Acorn Trail, and the Meadowlark Trail to the uphill(west) side of the preserve and then swing back to the parking lot via the Acorn and Perimeter trails.

The preserve is open daily from 8:00 a.m. until dusk. Unlike Foothills Park you don't need to be a Palo Alto resident to enjoy this preserve. For more information, call Foothills Park at (415) 329-2423.

Bicycle Access:
Bicycles are allowed on all trails except the Perimeter Trail.

Equestrian Access:
Horses are allowed on all trails

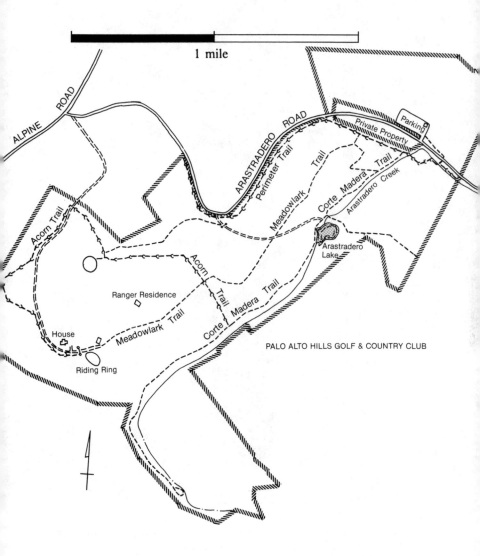

The Mother of the Forest tree is one of the redwood wonders along the Redwood Trail, an easy self-guiding nature loop near Big Basin park headquarters.

Big Basin Redwoods State Park

TO GET THERE... Take Highway 9 west from Skyline Boulevard and turn west on Highway 236. The southern access is from Boulder Creek.

Big Basin is a large and diverse land of dark redwood groves, sunny ridges, and rocky peaks. This is the largest park in the Santa Cruz Mountains, with enough miles of trails to satisfy the most enthusiastic of hikers. Here you will find more than 80 miles of trails, which allow hikers, bicyclists, and equestrians to escape the crowded paved areas and explore some of the mountains' most beautiful semi-wilderness.

The wildest and most spectacular hike in Big Basin is the 10.5-mile Skyline-to-the-Sea/Sunset trail loop to Berry Creek Falls. Take an entire day and enjoy the waterfalls and remote first-growth redwood groves, stopping often to appreciate the wonderful variety of scenery. This is not an easy hike, and it has plenty of ups and downs to encourage you to slow down and enjoy your rambles. The trail has a million rewards any time of year, but most people like it best in the late winter and early spring when everything is fresh and green and Berry Creek Falls is an awesome torrent, plunging more than 65 feet over mossy and fern-adorned sandstone cliffs. Upstream are Silver, Golden, and Cascade Falls.

This loop wanders far from the park's crowded paved areas and passes through all the region's ecological communities. To find this route, take the Redwood Trail past the campfire circle and across Opal Creek to the "Skyline-to-the-Sea" Trail, which connects with the Berry Creek and Sunset trails. Allow at least 6 hours of hiking to cover this trail. You can make a 2 day trip out of this route by camping at Sunset Trailcamp. It is about 5.5 miles from park headquarters.

The Howard King Trail can be taken as a longer and more strenuous alternative to a portion of the "Skyline-To-The-Sea" Trail. Take the Hihn Hammond dirt road up 1,840 foot high McAbee Mountain and turn right

(Continues on page 26)

Views of Waddell Canyon and the ocean are enjoyed from atop Mount McAbee.

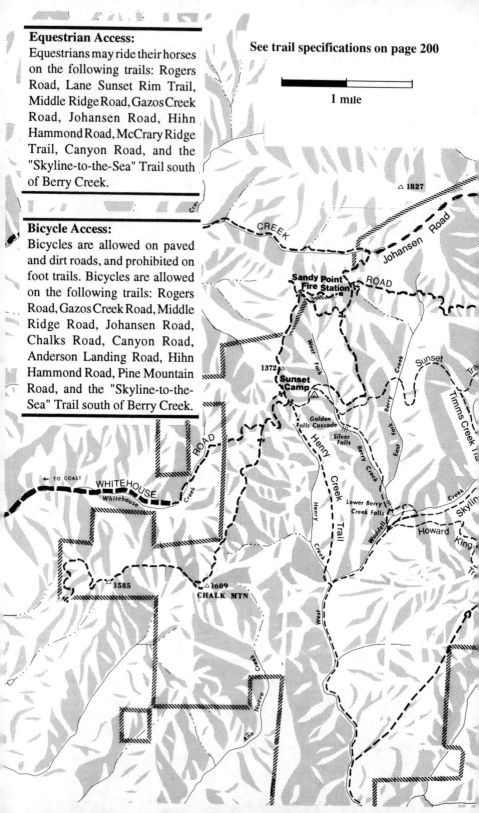

Equestrian Access:

Equestrians may ride their horses on the following trails: Rogers Road, Lane Sunset Rim Trail, Middle Ridge Road, Gazos Creek Road, Johansen Road, Hihn Hammond Road, McCrary Ridge Trail, Canyon Road, and the "Skyline-to-the-Sea" Trail south of Berry Creek.

Bicycle Access:

Bicycles are allowed on paved and dirt roads, and prohibited on foot trails. Bicycles are allowed on the following trails: Rogers Road, Gazos Creek Road, Middle Ridge Road, Johansen Road, Chalks Road, Canyon Road, Anderson Landing Road, Hihn Hammond Road, Pine Mountain Road, and the "Skyline-to-the-Sea" Trail south of Berry Creek.

See trail specifications on page 200

1 mile

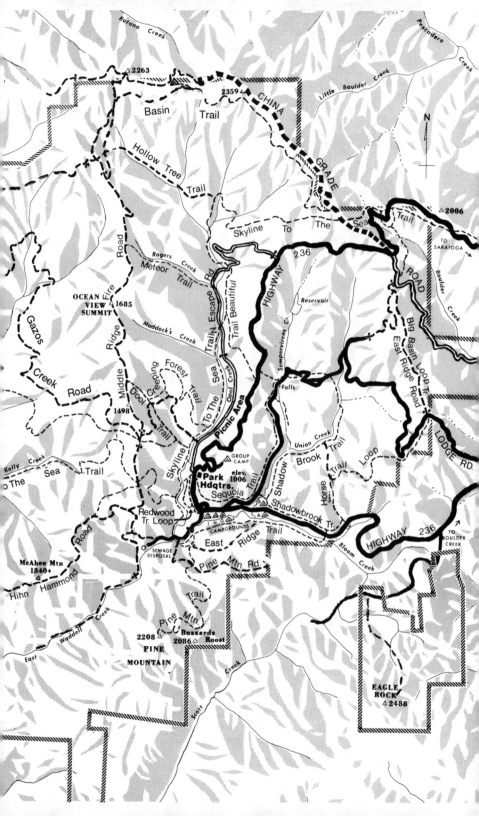

Silver Falls is one of a series of beautiful waterfalls in the Berry Creek Canyon.

(Continued from page 23)

on the trail. This route has some great views, especially of the Waddell Creek canyon to the southwest.

The trail to Pine Mountain and Buzzards Roost is a strenuous but scenic 5-mile round trip climb of more than 1,000 feet from park headquarters. The climb to the 2,208 foot summit of Pine Mountain is a journey above the redwoods to an ecological island of madrone, knobcone pine, and chapparal. The weathered sandstone summit of Buzzards Roost offers the best views of the two peaks. To take this hike from park headquarters, follow the "Skyline-to-the-Sea" Trail and Pine Mountain Road south and turn right on Pine Mountain Trail. Be sure to bring water, as there is none available on the peaks.

The knobcone pine is well suited for these dry and rocky ridgetops. It is found mostly in dry areas with poor soil, where most other trees do poorly. This hardy pine needs the direct sunlight of hilltops and ridges and is dependent on fire to remove competing vegetation and for generating sufficient heat to release seeds from the cones. You will also see knobcone pines on the Sunset Trail.

There is a strenuous one-day hike, or a moderate two-day backpacking trip on a scenic and diverse 14-mile loop trail through the park's northern mountains. From park headquarters walk the "Skyline-to-the-

Sea" Trail north and east to the Basin Trail, which climbs north and west to the Lane Sunset trailcamp. This is a spectacular place to spend a night, with a remote wilderness feel to it. Call park headquarters for reservations. To complete the loop follow the ridge westward to the Middle Ridge Trail, which is actually a dirt road. It follows a scenic ridge southbound, past Ocean View Summit. Take Sunset Trail east to the Skyline-to-the-Sea Trail and back to park headquarters. This hike passes through all the park's ecological zones and involves a climb of more than 1,300 feet. Don't forget to bring drinking water, especially in summer.

If that one is too tough, you might want to go to the other extreme and take the easiest trail in the park. Just west of the parking lot near park headquarters is Redwood Trail, an easy self-guiding nature loop by some of the largest trees in the park. The trail is less than a mile long and makes an easy family stroll.

Big Basin has a seasonal grocery store and a nature museum. Car camping and tent cabins may be reserved through Mistix at I (800) 444-7275. For more information call park headquarters at (408) 338-6132.

Rancho Del Oso

TO GET THERE. . . The entrance road intersects Highway I just north of Waddell Creek, about 18 miles northwest of Santa Cruz. Road access is for horse trailers and backpackers with reservations. All others use beach parking lot.

The southern part of Big Basin Redwoods State Park stretches all the way to the ocean, encompassing the broad valley of Waddell Creek. Called Rancho Del Oso (Spanish for "Ranch of the Bear"), this area offers a beautiful stream, forests of second-growth redwood, Douglas fir, and Monterey pine, as well as meadows and a freshwater marsh.

There are 3 easily accessible trail camps in this valley. Leave your car at the parking lot near the Rancho Del Oso office and backpack in about 1 mile to Alder Camp, 1.2 miles to Twin Redwoods Camp, and 2.5 miles to Camp Herbert. Sunset Camp is 6.8 miles. Make trail camp reservations by calling park headquarters at (408) 338-6132 at least 2 weeks in advance for summer weekend use. Ground fires are prohibited.

If you are taking the "Skyline-to-the-Sea" Trail from Big Basin park headquarters, the distance to Camp Herbert is 7.5 miles, Twin Redwoods is 9 miles, Alder Camp is 9.8 miles, and Highway 1 is about 11 miles.

Just south of Waddell Creek a narrow road leads to the Rancho del Oso Nature and History Center, where you can see natural and human history exhibits and join guided walks. The center is managed by the non-profit Waddell Creek Association in cooperation with the State Park system. There is an adjacent self-guided nature trail. The center is open Saturdays and Sundays 1-4 p.m. Guided nature walks are offered Sundays at 1 p.m.

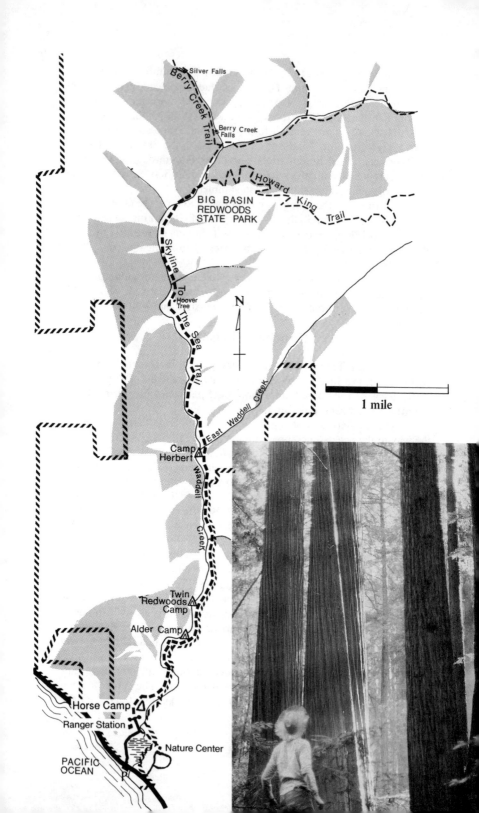

Silver Falls

Berry Creek Trail

Berry Creek Falls

Howard

King

Trail

BIG BASIN
REDWOODS
STATE PARK

Skyline

To Hoover Tree

N

To The Sea Trail

1 mile

East Waddell Creek

Camp Herbert

Waddell Creek

Twin Redwoods Camp

Alder Camp

Horse Camp

Ranger Station

Nature Center

PACIFIC OCEAN

This all-wood bridge, held together by wooden pegs, is on the trail to the top of Eagle Rock. There is limited parking at the trailhead on Little Basin Road, 1.3 miles from Highway 236.

SPECIAL SECTION

Rules of the Trail

These basic rules could go a long way toward encouraging harmony among trail users.

RUNNERS:
• *Alert hikers and equestrians before passing.*
• *Groups should run in single file.*

BICYCLISTS:
• *Approach each bend as if someone were around the corner.*
• *Alert hikers and joggers before passing.*
• *When approaching a horse from behind, stop and let the rider know you are there. Ask the rider if it is safe to pass.*
• *When approaching a horse face-to-face, stop and dismount if necessary.*

EQUESTRIANS:
• *Approach each bend as if someone were around the corner.*
• *Let other trail users know if your horse is safe to pass.*
• *Avoid muddy places. Deep hoof ruts are hard on other trail users.*

HIKERS:
• *Step to the side of the trail to let faster trail users pass.*
• *Groups should be careful not to block the trail.*

Bonny Doon Ecological Preserve

TO GET THERE. . . from Highway 1 take Bonny Doon Road to the town of Bonny Doon and turn south on Martin Road.

PLEASE NOTE: To protect endangered species and fragile habitat this preserve is open by permit only for organized groups and scientifc study. For a permit, contact the California Department of Fish and Came at (408) 649-2870.

This small area of strange sandstone formations and sandy soil is one of the most unique and interesting natural places in California.

It supports an extraordinary variety of unusual life, including the endangered Santa Cruz cypress tree, which exists in only a few groves, and the endangered Santa Cruz wallflower. The silver-leaved manzanita and Rattan's mimulus grow nowhere else in the world. You will also find a forest of stately ponderosa pine, a tree that is rarely seen in the coastal ranges, but common in the middle altitudes of the Sierra Nevada.

Also found here is the world's largest-known nesting site for the Colletes kincaidii, the solitary bee. Unlike other bees, which are highly social, the female solitary bee builds a single nest in the ground without help from other bees and then seals her eggs inside with a food supply. She then dies without encountering her offspring. This primitive bee is considered to be an evolutionary link between ancestral wasps and modern bees.

Other wildlife includes peregrine falcons, long-eared owls, Cooper's hawks, Santa Cruz kangaroo rats, golden eagles, purple martins, and California tiger salamanders.

What makes this 526-acre preserve a mecca for uniquely Californian plants and animals is its zayante sandstone outcroppings and sandy soil which is unique to Santa Cruz County. This geology is a remnant of uplifted ancient coastal sand dunes.

These sandstone formations are eroded into strangely beautiful shapes, different in form and texture from Castle Rock sandstone. From atop these outcrops are seen broad panoramas of mountains and ocean.

As unique as this ecosystem is, it is definitely not a wilderness. From the rocky summits houses are seen all around; and, in fact this land was acquired just in time before it was all subdivided and developed. Many years of off-road motorcycle abuse, garbage dumping, and graffitti carving on the sandstone have left this "biological island" a very sad sight.

It is the goal of the department of fish and game to restore the beauty and ecological integrity of this property. You can help by respecting access restrictions.

This preserve has a grove of ponderosa pines, which are rare in the Coast Range.

Burleigh Murray Ranch State Park

TO GET THERE. . . take Highway I just south of Half Moon Bay and turn east on Higgins Road. The dirt road trail into the park intersects Higgins Road next to "The Orchard Field", 1.6 miles from Highway 1.

Mills Creek tumbles more than a thousand feet down the steep western slopes of Cahill Ridge, at Skyline Boulevard, and then meanders through a broad and gentle valley as it approaches Higgins Road.

This perennial stream flows through the middle of this 1,325-acre state park, which is just 2 watersheds north of redwood-forested Purisima Creek Open Space Preserve. But unlike Purisima, the hills and mountains of Burleigh Murray are covered mainly with that combination of low bushes and vines known as coastal scrub, as well as with grasslands and scattered groves of eucalyptus. Creeks are clearly defined by narrow riperian woodlands.

Because this is ideal rabbit and rodent habitat, bobcats and coyotes abound. Birds of prey are commonly seen, including a variety of hawks and owls. Barn owls and swallows nest in the large dilapidated barn.

As of this writing, the only real trail in this park is the ranch road along Mills Creek, which is a well-maintained dirt road between Higgins Road and the house. Past the barn it more resembles a real trail, and beyond the water tanks it rapidly deteriorates, becoming progressively more difficult to follow through the scrub. There are several road cuts that have the potential of forming an excellent trail system once a route is cut through the brush. In addition to trails the park department also has plans for walk-in campsites.

From the Mills Creek ranch road you will see a cave in a sandstone outcropping high on the valley's south facing slope. It looks large and accessible from the trail, but a bushwhacking ordeal to near the ridgetop made me wish I had left my curiosity at home that day. I found the entrance to this shallow cave to be well-guarded by a steep and dangerous rocky slope.

For more information call (415) 726-8800.

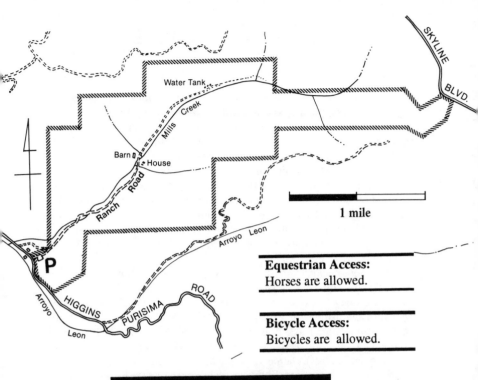

1 mile

Equestrian Access:
Horses are allowed.

Bicycle Access:
Bicycles are allowed.

SPECIAL SECTION

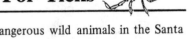

Watch Out For Ticks

Ticks are one of the most dangerous wild animals in the Santa Cruz Mountains.

These small blood-sucking arachnids wait on leaves and branches for victims to pass by. Once on board they excavate a hole in the skin and then excrete a powerful cement surrounding their mouthparts. There is about a 4 percent chance that the tick that bites you will be carrying Lyme disease, which is first detected by a circular red rash with a clear center that slowly expands. Later symptoms include fever, joint and muscle pain, fatigue, nausea, and headaches. This disease is most easily treated in its early stages.

BEFORE AN OUTING: *Wear snug-fitting clothes and apply insect repellent containing DEET, especially at the cuffs, neck, and waist.*

AFTER AN OUTING: *Inspect your body thoroughly. If you find a tick grab it with tweezers as close to the skin surface as possible and pull outward with steady, even pressure. Then disinfect the bite with isopropyl alcohol and wash hands with soap and water.*

Butano State Park

TO GET THERE . . . take Cloverdale Road about 3 miles east of Highway 1. The park is about 5 miles south of Pescadero.

It is hard to overstate the charm of this cool, green canyon park. It has a magical rain forest garden of redwoods and ferns cupped between steep ridges, which can be climbed for sweeping vistas.

The easiest hike in the park is on the Creek Trail which can be started on the left side of the road just before reaching the campfire center. This trail is short and mostly level and follows the heavily forested creek bed. More strenuous paths take hikers to the Olmo Fire Trail on the south ridge and the Butano Fire Trail on the north ridge. The Ano Nuevo Trail, stemming from the Olmo Trail, offers a view of Ano Nuevo Island and the ocean on clear days.

Serious backpackers should consider hiking the Olmo Fire Trail or the Jackson Flats Trail to Butano Trailcamp, which can be reached by following the Doe Ridge Trail up a gradual grade to the Olmo Fire Road. Then turn left on the Indian Trail and head about 200 yards to the Fire Road near the trailcamp. The Butano Fire Trail continues to the Jackson Flats Trail which returns to the park entrance area. This hike is about 5.5 miles each way and involves some vigorous hill climbing and a gain of about 1,400 feet to the trailcamp. Enthusiastic hikers may want to make a day of it and hike the loop in one day. Be sure to make reservations in advance to use the camp from May to October by calling park headquarters.

A few miles can be lopped off the loop by continuing on the Indian Trail into the canyon and on to the Jackson Flats Trail.

If you have truly extraordinary enthusiasm you may want to consider continuing on the Olmo Fire Trail all the way to Big Basin. The legality of hiking this route is still in doubt and camping is not permitted

See trail specifications on page 202

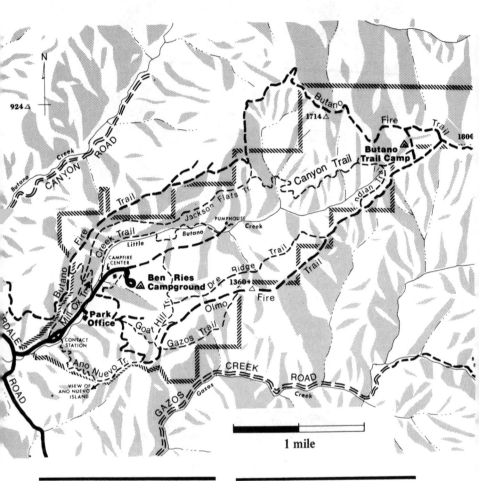

Bicycle Access:
Bicycles are allowed on the Olmo Fire Trail and the Butano Fire Trail.

Equestrian Access:
Horses are allowed on the Olmo Fire Trail and the Butano Fire Trail.

along the way.

For a good scenic 6-mile loop and an ideal moderate outing, combine the Goat Hill Trail, the Doe Ridge Trail, and the Olmo Fire Trail.

Butano State Park is a 2,200 acre enclave of redwoods in the coastal fog belt on the west side of the range. One of its joys is the absence of crowds. Because of its out of the way location you can often walk for hours without passing another hiker.

A free, ranger-guided bicycle tour of the park is offered. Reservations are required.

The Indians usually avoided the shady groves for both practical and religious reasons. They felt the same life force that many hikers still experience today, and were convinced that redwoods were haunted by powerful spirits. That wasn't the only reason they had to stay away, though. The main reason was that edible plants, for both man and deer, are rare in the redwood groves, and the Indians found happier hunting grounds elsewhere.

The park has 38 campsites, each with a table and stove and nearby restrooms. Reservations may be made through Mistix at 1 (800)444-7275.

For more information, call park headquarters at (415)879-0173.

SPECIAL SECTION

Poison Oak

The bad news is that poison oak is common in the Santa Cruz Mountains. But the good news is that it can be easily identified and the ill effects can normally only be acquired by physical contact with the plant. The only exception is by inhaling its smoke or by touching objects, pets, or people who have rubbed up against it. Fortunately for the 70 percent of the population that is at least mildly sensitive to the urushiol oil found in this shrub, contact is easily avoided. The Santa Cruz Mountains have many broad trails, including former ranch and logging roads, where you will be able to keep a safe distance.

If you do accidentally rub against poison oak leaves or stems (in winter some plants lack identifying leaves), a washing with soap and warm water will reduce the severity of the rash if done soon after contact.

Calero Reservoir County Park

TO GET THERE... from Highway 101 take Bernal Road west, Santa Teresa Boulevard south, and Bailey Avenue west.

This is one of the noisiest and quietest places in the Santa Cruz Mountains. The reservoir itself is noisy with urban refugees on summer weekends when the lake water is warm and inviting. Powerboats roar with pleasure, and this may seem the last place to find a little solitude.

A quick study of the map, however, reveals that most of this 2,284-acre park lies south of the reservoir and that a large area is now being enjoyed almost exclusively by equestrians and cows.

From Bailey, drive south on McKean a little under a mile to the entrance to Calero Farm. At the road that goes to the farm you will notice a wooden gate at the dirt road trail that loops through the park. Turn right on the first intersecting dirt road which passes a small pond and swings down to near the farm and then up and over the ridge. This route intersects the dirt road you started on and takes you back. The total distance is about 4 miles of easy walking. These generous grassy hills are kept trimmed by the persistent effort of grazing cattle, and are studded with park-like displays of oak, bay, and elderberry.

See trail specifications on page 202

Equestrian Access:
Horses are allowed on all trails.

Bicycle Access:
Bicycles are not permitted.

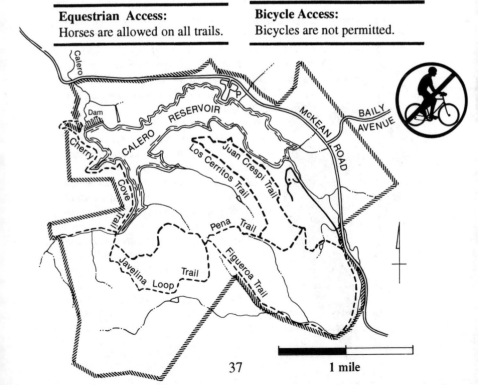

37   1 mile

On the dry southeast part of the Santa Cruz range, Calero has a pronounced split personality. From lush and green during the rainy season, to crisp and brown in the dry months, this park is worth visiting all through the year.

For more information call (408)268-3883.

Acorn Woodpeckers

When you see a dead tree trunk or branch riddled with holes and stocked with acorns then you have made yourself a guest in the territory of a colony of woodpeckers.

These raucous birds fill the air with a shrill "JACK-A jack-a" and are easily identified in flight by flashes of black and white on their wings and a glimmering red crown.

This is one of the few species of colonial woodpeckers, with all members of the community tending the eggs and young and digging out nesting holes in trees.

The most interesting time to watch these birds is in September and October when they gather acorns for winter provisions and wedge them tightly into holes in trees, fence posts, and even telephone poles so that squirrels can't pry them out. With binoculars you can easily see woodpeckers position the acorns pointed-end first into holes, and then lodge them in securely with a few good whacks with their beaks.

38

Cascade Ranch State Park

TO GET THERE. . . it is along Highway 1 just north and to the east of Año Nuevo State Reserve.

As of the time this edition goes to press this park is not yet ready for public use.

To get the latest access information call the state parks offices at (415)879-2025 or (415)726-8820.

This park is part of the historic 4,088-acre Cascade Ranch, which was saved from becoming a housing development by a coalition of public and private groups under the leadership of the Trust for Public Land, a non-profit organization based in San Francisco.

State legislation preserves about 2,500 acres as a state park; 700 acres for agricultural use with an easement to preclude development; and the remainder to be sold for use as a private campground and a public meeting center.

This park has several well-maintained dirt roads that would make excellent trails. Some abandoned old ranch roads that are overgrown with brush could be cleared and used as foot paths. The dirt road to Chalk Mountain begins among the gentle grassy cow pastures near the ranch buildings and makes a long ascent of the ridge. It climbs through shady forests of Douglas fir and second-growth redwood and onto the dry and rocky ridge where manzanita bush and the hardy knobcone pine abound. This trail goes to the top of Chalk Mountain, in Big Basin State Park, where you will enjoy a 360-degree panorama of the ocean, including Ano Nuevo Island. and vast areas of the Santa Cruz Mountains on a clear day. This route intersects Whitehouse Creek Road and passes through a wooded valley on its way back to Cascade Ranch.

With extraordinary diversity of habitat, including coastal scrub, ponds, Douglas fir, freshwater marsh, second-growth redwood, stream-

side vegetation, and grassland, this area supports an abundance of wildlife. Look for signs of deer, bobcat, coyote, and even mountain lion. Steelhead spawn in Gazos Creek during the rainy season. This is also where Monterey Pine reach the northernmost limit of their natural range.

The Cascade Ranch vicinity is rich in history and prehistory, going back ten thousand years. The Ohlone Indians thrived in this abundant land, feasting on acorns and other edible plants, deer and other game in the mountains, salmon and steelhead in the streams, and mussels, abalone, clams, and other bounty from the sea. Shellmounds attest to many centuries of gourmet dining.

Because of these ideal conditions this place was home to the largest settlement of Ohlone on the coast between Monterey and San Francisco. This is also the place where these Indians first made contact with Spanish explorer Gaspar de Portola during his long trek up the California coast in 1769.

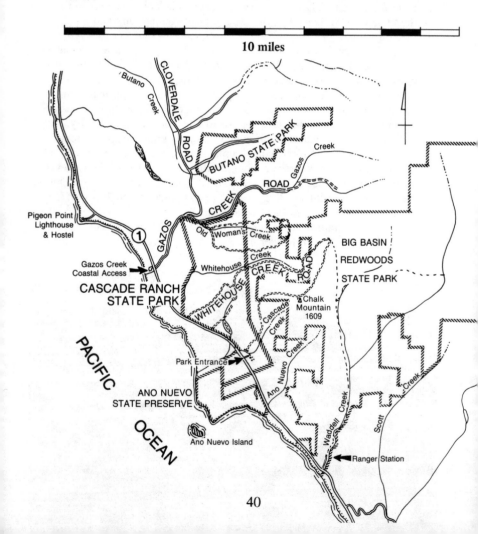

10 miles

Castle Rock State Park

TO GET THERE. . . take Skyline Boulevard about 2.6 miles south from its intersection with Highway 9 (Saratoga Gap).

Spectacular views in all directions, rock outcroppings ideal for climbing, waterfalls, and beautiful groves of oak, madrone, and Douglas fir make this one of my favorite parks.

Castle Rock itself is one of the Bay Area's most popular climbing rocks because of its challenging overhangs and impressive posture on the crest of the range. You can see the ocean and San Francisco Bay from the top. This 80-foot sandstone outcropping, however, is sometimes so congested that climbers must wait their turn to rappel off the summit.

This park covers 3,600 acres and has more than 30 miles of excellent trails. Hiking, picnicking, rock climbing, and backpacking are favorite activities here. To reach some of the outlying areas take the Ridge Trail heading uphill (north) from Saratoga Gap Trail east of the waterfall. Goat Rock, with its formidable south face for climbers, is easily ascended on the uphill side by hikers who marvel at the extraordinary views of Monterey Bay, the Monterey Peninsula, and the Santa Lucia Mountains 80 miles to the south. Continue west on the Ridge Trail for more views and lesser known rocks, and on to Castle Rock Trailcamp .

The Travertine Springs Trail offers a short cut to the "Skyline to the Sea" Trail and connects the eastern and western parts of the park. It takes a forested route, mainly through Douglas fir, bay, oak, and madrone woods.

This park has lots of great views.

Tafoni

The shallow caves and honeycomb texture (called "tafoni") in the sandstone outcroppings of the Santa Cruz Mountains are the result of what geologists call "cavernous weathering", a phenomenon that occurs only in a few places in the world.

First, there has to be outcroppings of sandstone cemented together with calcium carbonate in the form of mineral calcite. Next, the extent of cementation has to be variable, so that some parts of the rock are harder than others. And most importantly, this strange weathering only happens where there is a moderately dry climate with a prolonged dry season.

RAINY SEASON: OCTOBER to MAY

Rainwater with dissolved carbon dioxide seeps into rock

Castle Rock is less than half a mile south of the parking lot. The park's main trail, the Saratoga Gap Trail, begins at the opposite end of the parking lot from Skyline and continues through most of the park. About a mile from the parking lot is 100-foot Castle Rock Falls, which can be viewed from an observation platform.

A walk to Castle Rock Trailcamp, about 3.2 miles from the parking lot is a moderate 6.4- mile loop via the Ridge and Saratoga Gap trails. A shorter version of this loop can be made by taking the connecting trail between these two routes.

The Saratoga Gap Trail is on the west slope of the ridge, offering a wonderful chance to see the role of topography on mountain ecology. Compare the deep green of the moist evergreen valleys with the drought-resistant vegetation of the dry and rocky west and south facing ridgetops. Some of the most beautiful oak, madrone, and chaparral in the Santa Cruz Mountains are in this park.

From the trailcamp the Saratoga Gap Trail heads north to Saratoga Gap, at the intersection of Highway 9 and Skyline Boulevard; or you can take the Travertine Springs Trail to the "Skyline-to-the-Sea" Trail. Much

---

Heavy winter rains seep into the sandstone along cracks and planes of soft rock. The rain water contains carbon dioxide from the air, which dissolves the calcium carbonate that holds the sandstone grains together. The dry season allows the rock to dry out, and the calcium carbonate is then drawn to the surface by the capillary action of water. As the water evaporates, the calcium carbonate is left within a few feet of the surface to form a hard shield that resists erosion. The interior of the rock, however, is left without much cement and easily crumbles away and is removed by water, wind, and animal activity, including people.

Look for spheres of hard rock in the sandstone. These concretions are masses of complete rather than partial cementation. The reddish-brown color is the result of small amounts of iron oxide.

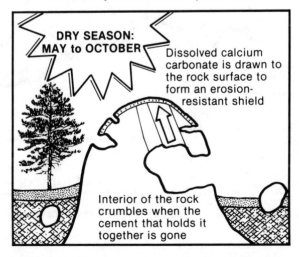

DRY SEASON: MAY to OCTOBER

Dissolved calcium carbonate is drawn to the rock surface to form an erosion-resistant shield

Interior of the rock crumbles when the cement that holds it together is gone

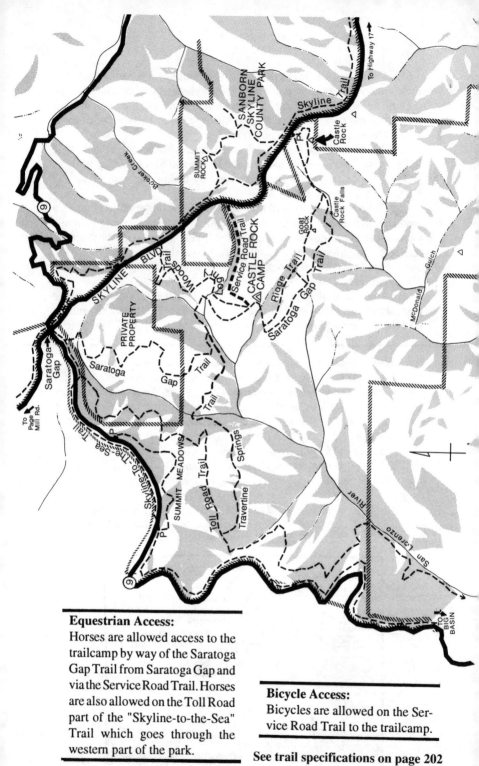

Equestrian Access:

Horses are allowed access to the trailcamp by way of the Saratoga Gap Trail from Saratoga Gap and via the Service Road Trail. Horses are also allowed on the Toll Road part of the "Skyline-to-the-Sea" Trail which goes through the western part of the park.

Bicycle Access:

Bicycles are allowed on the Service Road Trail to the trailcamp.

See trail specifications on page 202

of the park was acquired with the help of the Sempervirens fund (P.O. Box 1141, Los Altos, California 94022), which sells an excellent topographic map of this park. With its grassy promontories and Douglas fir, madrone, oak, and plenty of pleasing vistas, the Summit Meadows property may be explored by trail from Highway 9 west of Skyline Boulevard.

This park has an exceptional abundance and variety of spring wildflowers. The parking lot area is a good place to look for the exotically beautiful spotted coral root, a member of the orchid family that has no green, chlorophyll-producing parts. It absorbs energy from decaying organic material in the soil. Grasslands explode with vibrant displays of mule ear, buttercup, baby blue eyes, larkspur, iris, and many others. Because of its higher elevation you can continue enjoying native flowers here long after they have wilted in lower parks. Chaparral blooms with monkey flower, chaparral pea, ceanothus, pitcher sage, and bush poppy, to mention a few.

Because this park can get hot and dry be sure to carry water. Sturdy footwear will come in handy on the rocky sections of trail.

The park's trailcamp has 25 sites, available on a first-come, first-served basis. Water is available. A ranger told me that it has never been filled to capacity. For more information, call park headquarters at (408)338-6132 or (408)867-2952..

SPECIAL SECTION

Help Build A Trail

Every spring since 1969, volunteers have hit the trails of the Santa Cruz Mountains with shovels, picks, and trimmers to undo winter's damage and to build new trails. This tradition has been so successful that it is the model for a similar statewide event.

With tight budgets for public agencies, Trail Days-and smaller trail projects throughout the year-are essential to keeping these mountains accessible.

Coordinating these trail activities is The Trail Center, a coalition of organizations including the Sempervirens Fund, The Santa Cruz Mountains Trail Association, the Midpeninsula Regional Open Space District, and state and county parks departments.

If you would like to help, contact the Center at 4898 El Camino Real, Office 205A, Los Altos, CA 94022; (415) 968-7065.

A PIONEER LEGEND

Mountain Charley

Born in 1812, Charley McKiernan left hard times in his native Ireland for a life of adventure. After serving with the British army in Australia he headed for the unsettled wilds of California.

In 1850 Charley built a small cabin and raised sheep near the Skyline summit between Santa Clara and Santa Cruz counties. Back in those days the Santa Cruz Mountains were still wild and remote. Grizzly bears were still common, and they discovered that sheep were easy to catch and good to eat.

Considering grizzlies to be vermin, Charley made a name for himself as a bear hunter. In 1854 he and a friend made the mistake of sneaking up on a sow bear with 2 cubs. When she charged, Charley fired his rifle, but only wounded the bear. In the hand-to-hand combat that followed, Mountain Charley swung his muzzle loader at the bruin until it broke. After the bear left him for dead his friends carried the unconscious mountain man back to his cabin.

That grizzly cost Charley his left eye and left a gaping hole in his skull that a San Jose doctor covered with a flattened Mexican silver dollar. For many years to come he was embarrassed enough about the silver plate to wear his hat cocked over his forehead.

In 1862, at the age of 50, Charley married Barbara Bercary and they raised 7 children in their cabin. He died in 1892 at the age of 80.

Today, Charley is memorialized by Mountain Charley Road, which he helped build as a toll road, and by the Mountain Charley Tree, a large redwood near Glenwood.

MOUNTAIN CHARLEY GRABBED HIS GUN... AND HUNTED GRIZZLY BEARS FOR FUN... 'TILL ONCE HE FIRED, BUT MISSED INSTEAD... AND GRIZ BIT A HOLE IN CHARLEY'S HEAD

Coal Creek Open Space Preserve

TO GET THERE... park at the vista point on Skyline Boulevard 1.1 miles north of Page Mill Road and walk down the road that intersects Skyline just to the north. Another access is at the intersection of Skyline and Crazy Pete's Road, 1.8 miles north of Page Mill Road. To visit the Mount Melville area, park on Skyline just north of where it intersects Langley Hill Quarry Road.

This 476-acre preserve slopes eastward from Skyline Boulevard to form a pleasant place to ramble on about 4 miles of ranch roads. As of this writing, however, preserve boundaries and trails are not clearly identified. Be aware that it is easy to get lost if you are not careful.

A pleasant 2.6-mile loop can be taken from the Vista point on Skyline down to Alpine Road to the northeast, where it intersects Crazy Pete's Road and then climbs back to Skyline. On the Crazy Pete's Road trail, just uphill from Alpine Road, a footbridge crosses a beautiful cascading series of waterfalls that is particularly impressive during the rainy season. The area is covered with oak, bay, some very large madrone, and grasslands. A clear day will reveal some great views of the south Bay Area.

The easy walk up Mount Melville, southwest of where Skyline Boulevard intersects Langley Hill Quarry Road, is rewarded by spectacular views of the Santa Cruz Mountains vicinity, stretching well out to sea to the west and to the bay and beyond to the east. Most of the hill is open grassland, but at the top is a stately grove of oak, bay, and madrone that offers shelter from the wind and sun.

For more information contact the Midpeninsula Regional Open Space District at (415)691-1200. **SEE MAP ON PAGE 128**

Duveneck Windmill Pasture Area
(Rancho San Antonio Open Space Preserve)

TO GET THERE... take Moody Road west past Foothill College in Los Altos Hills, and turn left on Rhus Ridge Road. Park at the gate near a tennis court. It can also be reached by way of Hidden Villa Ranch.

Rising through the foothills of the Santa Cruz Mountains and up the steep Monte Bello Ridge, this 880-acre park has close urban proximity for casual day walks and access to adjoining parks for more strenuous outings.

From the gate, hike the short but steep dirt road to the top of the ridge. This stretch of trail is strenuous, but the rewards are great and the grade levels out when you reach the ridgetop, with wonderful panoramas of the hills and mountains to the west, including Black Mountain. At the top of the ridge the trail forks in 3 directions. Take the middle route, which heads west through the oak-studded grasslands and then swings south for a view of an old metal windmill in a grassy clearing.

A vigorous and spectacular 3.5-mile trail climbs 2380 feet to the summit of Black Mountain, in Monte Bello Open Space. By arranging a car shuttle you can walk about 7 scenic and inspiring miles from Windmill Pasture, up Black Mountain, and north on Monte Bello Ridge to Page Mill Road. A trailcamp near Black Mountain allows the trip to be broken into 2 days and allows the rare opportunity to camp in the grasslands east of Skyline. Fire is prohibited and reservations are required.

The Windmill Pasture was part of the 2,300-acre Hidden Villa Ranch, which was owned by Frank and Josephine Duveneck between 1923 and 1977, when they gave it to the public as a preserve. The windmill is a remnant of the generations of ranching in these hills. Just west of the preserve is Hidden Villa Ranch, famous for its Youth Hostel and environmental education programs.

See the Hidden Villa chapter for more information

This preserve has about 6 miles of trails. It is classified as part of the Rancho San Antonio Open Space Preserve, which can be reached by trail to the east. For further information, call the Midpeninsula Regional Open Space District at (415) 691-1200.

Equestrian Access:
Horses are allowed on all trails, though the Black Mountain Trail may be closed seasonally after rain.

Bicycle Access:
Bicycles are not permitted.

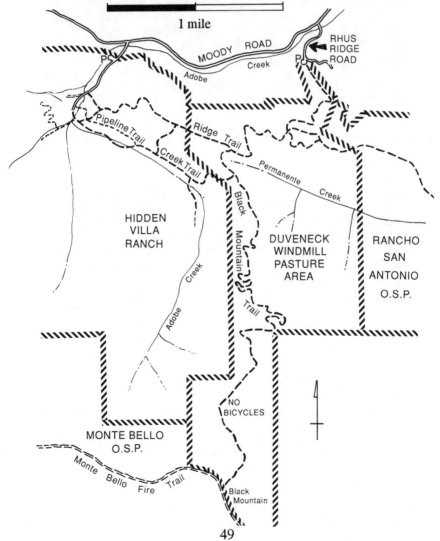

1 mile

RHUS RIDGE ROAD

MOODY ROAD

Adobe Creek

P

P

Pipeline Trail

Ridge Trail

Creek Trail

Permanente Creek

Black Mountain Trail

HIDDEN VILLA RANCH

Adobe Creek

DUVENECK WINDMILL PASTURE AREA

RANCHO SAN ANTONIO O.S.P.

NO BICYCLES

MONTE BELLO O.S.P.

Monte Bello Fire Trail

Black Mountain

Edgewood County Park & Preserve

TO GET THERE ... the main entrance is on Edgewood Road at Old Stagecoach Road opposite Crestview Drive. Other accesses are at Edgewood Road just east of Highway 280 across from the parking lot; and at the intersection of Hillcrest Way and Sunset in Redwood City.

The grasslands of this 467-acre park are famous for some of the Bay Area's most spectacular displays of springtime wildflowers. Because of its easy access to the Redwood City area, this is a wonderful place for picnics and short walks that take only a few hours out of the day.

The park's serpentine grasslands support 7 rare and endangered plant species and the endangered Bay Checkerspot Butterfly. Serpentine, associated with fault zones, provides poor soil for non-native plants because of its high toxicity and low water-holding capacity, but encourages the growth of indigenous flowering plants in great abundance. In April look for dazzling displays of goldfields, blue-eyed grass, tidy tips, and buttercups, to name a few.

Edgewood has about 8 miles of clearly-marked trails, popular with walkers and equestrians, that climb the forested 800-foot ridge and circle the grassland perimeter. The Edgewood access trail paralleling Edgewood Road connects with the Crystal Springs Trail and on to Huddart Park and from there on to Wunderlich Park and Purisima Creek Open Space.

For more information call (415) 363-4021.

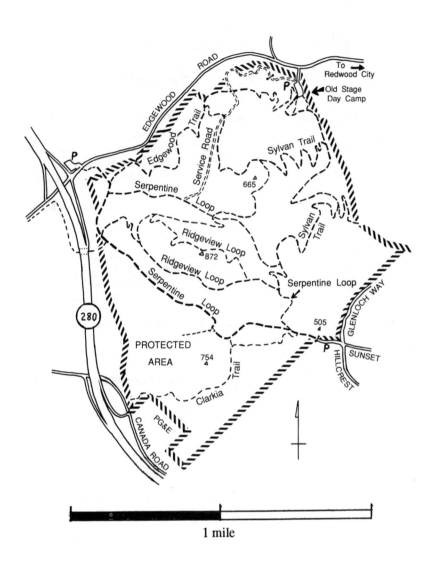

1 mile

Equestrian Access:
Horses are allowed on all trails, subject to closure when wet.

Bicycle Access:
Bicycles are not permitted.

See trail specifications on page 202.

El Corte de Madera Creek
Open Space Preserve

    TO GET THERE. . . from Highway 92 take Skyline Boulevard south 8.6 miles to the Caltrans Rest Stop at Skegg's Point. It is 3 .9 miles north of Woodside Road. From Skegg's Point walk north about a quarter of a mile to where two roads intersect at Skyline and take the dirt road to the right. There is another access half a mile south of Skegg's Point, across from the Methuselah Tree.

    At the headwaters of El Corte de Madera Creek, this 2,789-acre preserve combines scenic ridgetops and ocean views with deep verdant valleys filled with second-growth redwood and Douglas fir.

Equestrian Access:	Bicycle Access:
Horses are allowed on all trails except the footpath to the sandstone formation.	Bicycles are allowed on all trails except the footpath to the sandstone formation.

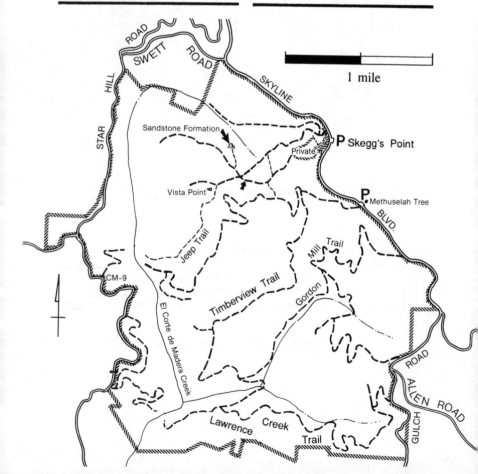

This preserve's most popular attraction is a spectacular sandstone formation with shallow caves and honeycomb depressions reminiscent of outcroppings at Castle Rock State Park, though it seems to be made of a softer and more fragile material. For this reason climbing is not allowed. You will find a description of how these features were formed in the Castle Rock chapter. The rock is 2.5 miles from the trailhead near Skegg's Point.

Some spectacular views are revealed along the ridgetop near the rock, especially at Vista Point, where low brush allows a good panorama to the south and west, stretching way out to sea on a clear day. This is a fine place for a lunch break, wind and fog permitting.

The trails in this preserve are old logging roads.

For more information and a current trail map call the Midpeninsula Regional Open Space District at (415) 691-1200.

The process of cavernous weathering (SEE PAGE 42) has created shallow caves and strange honeycomb patterns in the rock.

El Sereno Open Space Preserve

TO GET THERE... from Highway 17 take Montevina Road 3 miles west to its end where a turnout provides parking for a few cars.

This 1,083-acre preserve spans 2 miles of scenic ridgetop and steep canyons on the east side of the range. Chaparral covers most of the area, with oak, madrone, and bay scattered through the area, providing islands of shade for summer visitors. Beautiful groves of madrone and bay grow on the north and east sides of the ridge.

A good time to visit is in early spring, when chamise, ceanothus and other chaparral vegetation burst forth with new growth and are adorned with an abundance of flowers. Use your nose often here to appreciate the spicy aromas that offer a special appeal in this kind of plant community. You will see and hear lots of birds as they feed off the many seeds and berries that grow here.

Another advantage of chaparral is that it is low enough that it doesn't obstruct the commanding vistas of the Santa Cruz Mountains and the urbanized Santa Clara Valley. To the north you will see Black Mountain, Oakland, and even Mount Tamalpais, and to the southeast

Equestrian Access:
Horses are allowed on all trails.

Bicycle Access:
Bicycles are allowed on all trails.

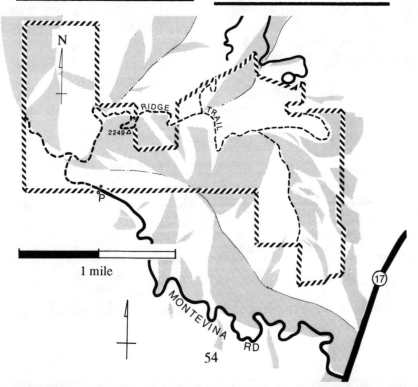

1 mile

stands Mount Umunhum. The views are particularly stunning on those cold crystal clear days of winter when the smog and haze are gone from the valley below.

Most of the trails through this park are dirt roads, and if you have ever tried cross-country hiking through chaparral you will appreciate why this is a good place for sticking to the established trails. Hikers should also be aware that this is one of the region's driest parks and water should be carried. Animals you might see here include woodrats, black-tail deer, rabbits, and coyotes.

This park is open for day use only. For more inforrnation, call the Midpeninsula Regional Open Space District at (415) 691-1200.

SPECIAL SECTION

Santa Cruz Mountains Geology

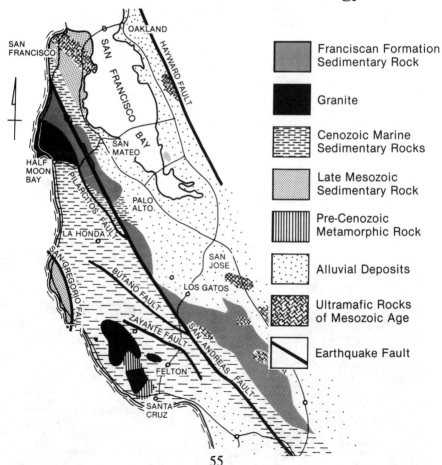

Franciscan Formation Sedimentary Rock

Granite

Cenozoic Marine Sedimentary Rocks

Late Mesozoic Sedimentary Rock

Pre-Cenozoic Metamorphic Rock

Alluvial Deposits

Ultramafic Rocks of Mesozoic Age

Earthquake Fault

Filoli Estate

TO GET THERE. . . from Highway 280, take Edgewood Road west and turn right on Canada Road.

The magniflcent Georgian-style mansion and adjoining 27 landscaped acres are one of San Mateo County's premier tourist attractions. What many visitors don't realize is that the undeveloped majority of the estate, which climbs all the way up the ridge to Skyline Boulevard, is also worth exploring.

Be aware that this is not a public park. It is owned by the National Trust for Historic Preservation and is accessible only through docent-led group tours. All walks are by advance reservations only and there is a fee.

Nature walks are offered weekdays and saturday mornings, visiting the Ohlone Indian dig, an excellent museum of Indian and Natural history, the San Andreas Fault, a small reservoir, and the Bourn family cemetery. The 728-acre estate has a wonderful variety of habitats, including grasslands, oakwoods, second-growth redwoods, and chaparral. It is ideal wildlife habitat and seems to be a particularly good place to see birds of prey.

The liesurely 2 1/2-hour nature walks cover about 3 miles. Groups of ten or more may arrange for private, personalized walks.

The name "Filoli" comes from the Bourn family motto: "To Fight, To Love, To Live." The mansion was built in 1917 for Mr. and Mrs. William B. Bourn II and was their home until they died in 1936. A walking tour of the mansion and gardens takes about 2 hours and is not available to children under 12 years of age. House and garden tours are conducted Tuesdays through Saturdays from mid-February until mid-November. Advance reservations are necessary and there is an admission charge.

For more information about nature hikes and house and garden tours call Friends of Filoli at (415) 364-2880, Monday through Friday 9 a.m. to 3 p.m.

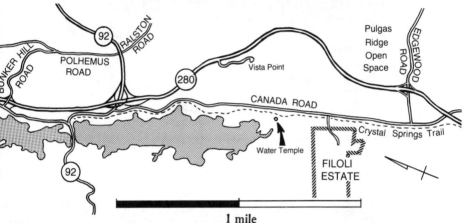

1 mile

Foothills Open Space Preserve

TO GET THERE. . . it is on the south side of Page Mill Road, about a mile uphill from the entrance to Foothills Park. Enter at a brown metal gate.

This small preserve is covered mainly with chaparral and oak. From the Page Mill Road entrance an easy half-mile trail goes to a rounded grassy knoll with a wide view of the southern Bay Area. A very steep trail continues on down to Hidden Villa Ranch.

This is one of the open space preserves where dog walking is allowed. Be sure to keep your pet on a leash.

Because of limited parking you are encouraged to call the Midpeninsula Regional Open Space District at (415) 691-1200 before visiting .

Foothill Park

TO GET THERE... take Page Mill Road in Palo Alto west of Highway 280.

The city of Palo Alto operates a 1,400- acre "nature preserve" in the low foothills west of town. The park, on the steep eastern slopes of the Santa Cruz Mountains, is characterized by grasslands, chaparral, oak, madrone, bay, buckeye, and a big lawn and picnic area. You may also appreciate the small reservoir for fishing near the park entrance and the nature interpretive center, near the lawn, that has an educational exhibit of native plants and animals.

These wide, grassy expanses are inhabited by multitudes of ground squirrels and the birds of prey which feed on them. Many species of birds are easily seen here—so bring binoculars.

The park changes from season to season and is pleasant for hiking all year, though my favorite time is the green, flowering months of early spring. The preserve has about 15 miles of hiking trails, including several scenic loops of 5 to 7 miles, with some nice vistas of the south Bay Area.

Unfortunately for most Bay Area explorers this park is open only to Palo Alto residents and their guests, and you will be asked for identification at the gate. For information about the regularly scheduled nature walks, call park headquarters at (415) 329-2423.

The park is open for day use only.

Coyote

Forest of Nisene Marks State Park

TO GET THERE. . . take the Aptos Creek Road north from Soquel Drive in Aptos.

The Forest of Nisene Marks is a vast and rugged semi-wilderness, with few of the facilities we normally expect from state parks. It's a diverse land of redwood forests, riperian woodlands, oak groves, stands of knobcone pine, and chaparral; and it has a robust pioneer history whose remnants are rotting away and becoming part of the landscape.

This park has lots of trails for hiking and bicycling through some beautiful forest scenery. Camping is permitted only at the trailcamp near the Sand Point Overlook, which is 6 miles by way of the West Ridge Trail from the Aptos Creek Road trailhead. It can also be reached by hiking or biking 5.4 miles up Buzzard Lagoon Road and the Aptos Creek Fire Road past the locked gate off Eureka Canyon Road.

In the 1880's Southern Pacific built a broad-guage railroad line up Aptos Creek to log this area. Then the Loma Prieta Lumber Company built the largest lumber mill in Santa Cruz County and a company town that included a telegraph office, hotel, and school. When the last of the old-growth redwood was cut in the 1920's a total of 140 million board feet of lumber had been removed.

The Loma Prieta Grade and West Ridge trails wind through some steep terrain and can be strenuous for beginners; but the entire loop is only about 7 miles and at an easy pace almost anyone should be able to make it. You can hike north on the West Ridge Trail to the trailcamp. Watch out for poison oak in this area.

A strenuous loop hike of more than 19 miles, and a gain of more than 1,000 feet, can be achieved by combining the Aptos Creek Fire Road with

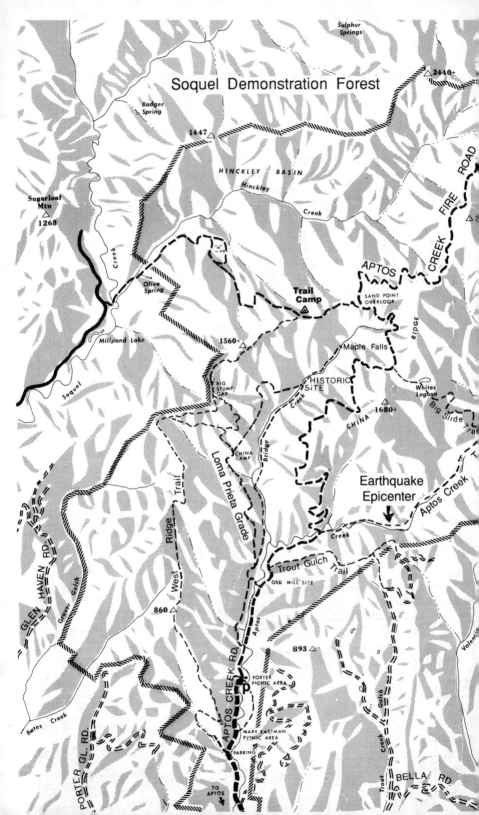

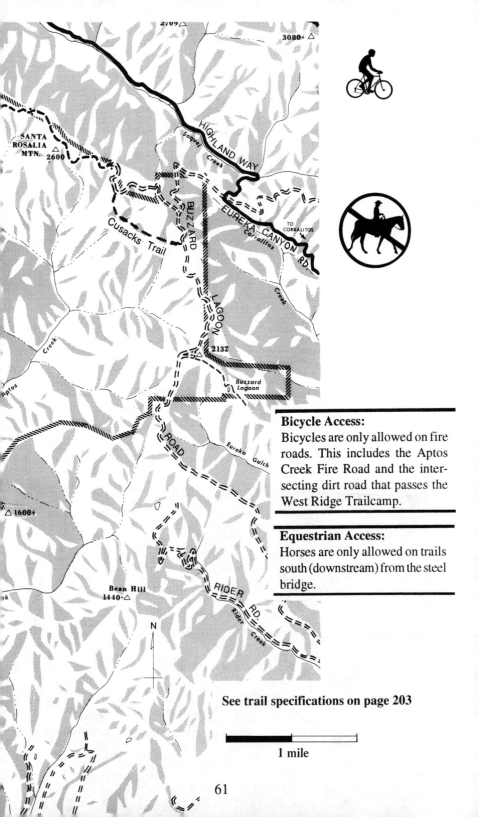

Bicycle Access:
Bicycles are only allowed on fire roads. This includes the Aptos Creek Fire Road and the intersecting dirt road that passes the West Ridge Trailcamp.

Equestrian Access:
Horses are only allowed on trails south (downstream) from the steel bridge.

See trail specifications on page 203

1 mile

61

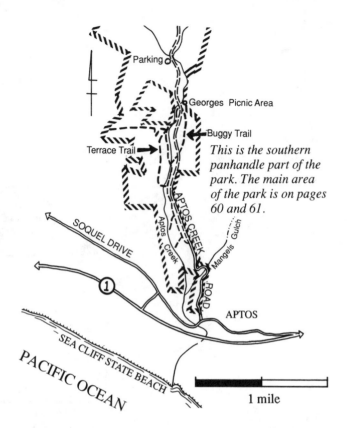

Parking

Georges Picnic Area

Buggy Trail

Terrace Trail

This is the southern panhandle part of the park. The main area of the park is on pages 60 and 61.

APTOS CREEK

Aptos Creek

Mangels Gulch

ROAD

SOQUEL DRIVE

①

APTOS

SEA CLIFF STATE BEACH

PACIFIC OCEAN

1 mile

The epicenter of the big October 17, 1989 earthquake was in this park. On the Big Slide Trail this and other fissures testify to the power of the quake.

West Ridge Trail and Loma Prieta Grade. Despite the long uphill grade, the Aptos Creek Fire Road will reward you with views of the surrounding mountains and occasionally the ocean. Fossil seashells are common in the exposed road cuts as this route climbs above the redwoods and into oak, madrone, and chaparral.

The park covers more than 10,000 acres and all the creeks that flow through it originate within its boundaries. These brawling arteries of life support their own plant communities and have vertical gardens of five finger ferns hanging from their moist, shady banks.

You can reach Nisene Marks by trail from Mount Madonna and Uvas Canyon county parks. From both parks, walk the Summit Road to the Ormsby Cut-off (unpaved and gated roads); cross the Eureka Canyon Road and take unpaved Buzzard Lagoon Road to the gated entrance to Forest of Nisene Marks State Park. From here it is a little over 6 miles to the park's trail camp.

The distance between Nisene Marks and Uvas canyon is 12 strenuous miles. It is 16 miles to Mount Madonna.

The park is open daily from 6 a.m. until sunset. Perhaps because horses are not allowed this has become the most popular mountain bike park in the Santa Cruz Mountains. Offroad bicycles are only allowed on designated dirt roads.

This park has lots of trails for hiking and bicycling through some beautiful forest scenery. Camping is permitted only at the trailcamp near the Sand Point Overlook,which is 6 miles by way of the West Ridge Trail from the Aptos Creek Road trailhead. It can also be reached by hiking or biking 5.4 miles up Buzzard Lagoon Road and the Aptos Creek Fire Road past the locked gate off Eureka Canyon Road.

For further information and trailcamp reservations, call (408) 335-4598 or (408)688-3222 or write: Henry Cowell Redwoods State Park, 101 North Big Trees Park Road, Felton, CA 95018.

Fremont Older Open Space Preserve

TO GET THERE... From Saratoga-Sunnyvale Road, take Prospect Road west to the end of the road. A trail into the park can also be taken from the Villa Maria area of Stevens Creek County Park off Stevens Canyon Road.

This 734-acre foothill preserve near Cupertino is an easy land of gentle hills and leisurely walks. The 7 miles of trails ramble through oakwoods, grasslands, chaparral, hayfields, and remnant walnut and apricot groves that still bear fruit. Since 1870 this land has produced grapes, apricots, prunes, walnuts, and olives.

This park is a gentle blend of natural and agricultural qualities; but it still hosts a wonderful abundance of wildlife. Deer roam freely, squirrels trapeze across the green leafy forest canopy, and woodpeckers tap holes in oak trees.

There is a pleasurable 3-mile loop walk from the parking lot, up to a scenic hilltop and around the Seven Springs Loop Trail and back. This moderately easy saunter takes you up Hunters Point and then downhill along the loop. The Seven Springs loop trail is named for the many springs that once provided water for nearby agriculture. The abandoned apricot groves along the way bear fruit around late June.

For a fairly strenuous 7.5 mile workout, with some steep ups and downs and some extraordinary views, take a grand loop through this preserve and into the adjoining Stevens Creek County Park. From the parking lot at the end of Prospect Road head uphill and to the west, turn right on the Ridge Trail and follow it up the ridge and down the other side into Stevens Creek County Park. Turn left on the Lakeside Trail and on

Stevens Canyon Trail and back up into Fremont Older via the Lookout Trail.

The home of distinguished San Francisco newspaper editor Fremont Older, which was originally built in 1911, has been faithfully restored and is open to the public occasionally for group tours. The property was purchased by the Midpeninsula Regional Open Space District in 1975, and the house is under private lease.

The preserve is open from dawn to dusk and fire arms and motor vehicles are prohibited. Be sure to carry water, especially during the summer months. Most of the park's trails are dirt ranch roads. For more information, call the Midpeninsula Regional Open Space District at (415) 691-1200.

Dogs on leashes are allowed in designated areas.

Equestrian Access:
Horses are allowed on all trails except the short footpath near the Prospect Road entrance.

Bicycle Access:
Bicycles are allowed on all trails except the short footpath near the Prospecrt Road entrance.

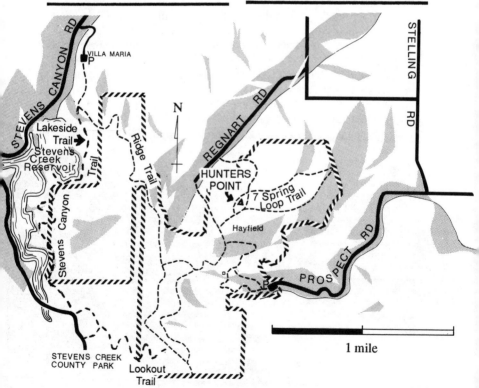

Golden Gate National Recreation Area

SWEENEY RIDGE

TO GET THERE ... from Highway 280 in San Bruno, take Sneath Lane west to a locked gate. The road continues as a trail. The park is also accessible from the south side of Skyline College, which is at the end of College Drive, off Skyline Boulevard in San Bruno. A dirt road runs south from the college to Sweeney Ridge. From Pacifica take Highway 1 south of Sharp Park to Shelldance Nursery. Continue up the driveway past the nursery to a wide dirt lot. Park there and walk up the fire road past the locked gate.

This is a place to go for breathtaking Bay Area views and spring wildflowers. On a clear day you can see the Pacific Ocean, the Farallon Islands, Mount Tamalpais, San Bruno Mountain, Mount Diablo, San Francisco Bay, Mount Hamilton, Moffett Field, San Andreas Lake, and many cities ringing the bay. This is a good place to become familiar with Bay Area geography.

Of course, these spectacular views can only be seen on clear days; and when the ridge is shrouded in ocean fog trail users can easily become disoriented, and even lost.

From the gate on Sneath Lane, the trail climbs about 600 feet and 1.9 miles to the Portola Discovery Site at an elevation of 1280 feet. The road itself is on national park land, but both sides are in the San Francisco watershed, where public access is prohibited. The actual discovery site is marked by 2 stone monuments, one to Portola, and another dedicated to the late conservationist Carl McCarthy.

At this place, on November 4, 1769, Captain Gaspar de Portola, seeking Monterey Bay, accidentally found the large arm of the ocean which was named San Francisco Bay. Portola thought that this inland sea

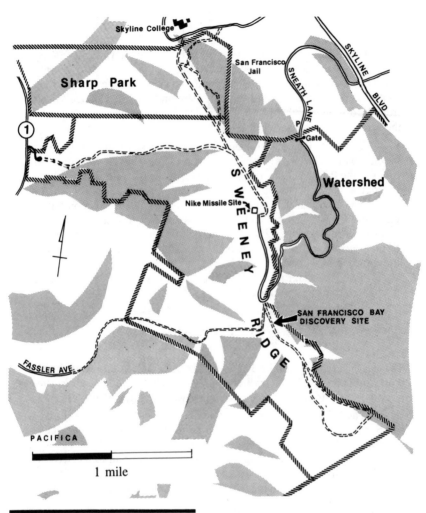

Equestrian Access:
Horses are allowed on the fire roads and the horse trail from the Linda Mar stables. There is no horse access via Sneath Lane.

Bicycle Access:
Bicycles are allowed on paved and dirt roads.

was Drakes Bay, near Point Reyes, and was disappointed to have missed Monterey Bay. After returning to San Diego he realized that this bay, one of the world's best natural harbors, was a new discovery and a perfect place for a Spanish presidio.

Covering 1047 acres, Sweeney Ridge is covered mostly with coastal scrub and grasses. Wildflowers are abundant in April and May, including checkermallow, Indian paintbrush, lupine, colombine, and blue-eyed grass. This is also an excellent place to see a wide variety of birds.

From near the discovery site, the Sneath Lane trail veers sharply north and ends at an abandoned Nike missile site. From here, a dirt road continues north and downhill to Sharp Park and Skyline College. South from the discovery site a dirt road traces the ridgetop to the boundary with the watershed property, which is off limits.

The Mori Ridge Trail from Highway 1 makes a steep 1,600-foot ascent up the ridge with lots of ocean views. You can take this route 2.5 miles to the Portola Discovery Site. The distance is 2 miles from Skyline College to the Discovery Site with an elevation gain of 500 feet.

The National Park Service offers ranger-guided walks on Saturdays dealing with natural and human history. Rangers also lead walks from Fassler Avenue in Pacifica. As of this writing this route passes through private property and is only accessible with ranger escort. For more information, call (415) 556-8371.

Sweeney Ridge is often foggy, and usually windy, especially in the afternoon; so dress appropriately.

FORT FUNSTON

TO GET THERE. . . from Highway 280 take John Daly Boulevard west and turn north on Skyline Boulevard (Highway 35). It's in the southwest corner of San Francisco, just west of Lake Merced.

The hills of San Francisco are actually the northernmost foothills of the Santa Cruz Mountains. At Fort Funston you can see the only part of this city that is still anything close to its natural condition.

Covered with sand dunes, as most of western San Francisco was originally, this 116-acre area was spared from development by the army in the early 1900's. Named for General Frederick Funston, a hero of the

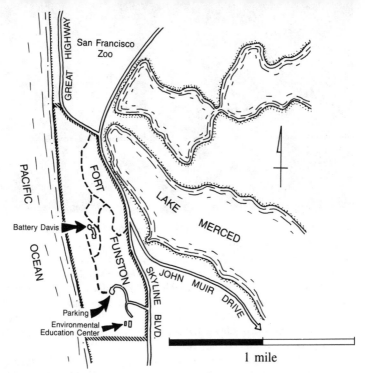

1 mile

Spanish-American War, the fort was established to help defend the coast against foreign invasion.

Fort Funston is ideal for easy walks and for exploring relics of military history. It also has a wheelchair-accessible paved trail. Be sure to watch for hang gliders soaring along the bluffs above the beach.

PHLEGER ESTATE

TO GET THERE... In Woodside, the estate is just north of Huddart County Park and just east of Skyline Boulevard.

PLEASE NOTE: As of this writing, the Phleger property is in the process of being acquired. For current access information, call the Golden Gate National Recreation Area at (415)556-8371.

This 1,257-acre unit of the Golden Gate National Recreation Area is a mixture of second-growth redwoods, oak, bay, big-leaf maple, and madrone.

This acquisition, with the only redwood forest in the GGNRA, will tie together many public lands to form an unbroken greenbelt from Sweeney Ridge to the north all the way through the San Francisco watershed property to Huddart, Wunderlich, and Edgewood County Parks. It is also one of the last remaining Santa Cruz Mountains links in the Bay Area Ridge Trail. It will allow the Ridge Trail to parallel Skyline Boulevard up on the ridge.

This property can be reached from adjacent Huddart County Park. From the Zwierleim Picnic Area take Zwierleim Trail, turn left (North) on Richard's Road Trail, right (East) on the trail to Woodside, and left (North)

on the Miramontes Trail in the Phleger Estate. See the Huddart County Park chapter on page 80.

There is an existing trail system through this estate built long ago by equestrian clubs. Look for metal trail markers depicting an Indian on a horse placed by equestrians in the 1930's. Plans call for expanding this trail system, emphasizing low-intensity use by equestrians and walkers. Parking will be improved and interpretive stations may be added. A main access will be from Skyline Boulevard. It is even possible that spawning steelhead trout can be reintroduced into West Union Creek.

The Phleger Estate was clearcut in the 1860's and '70's. Redwood lumber was shipped out of Redwood City for the building of San Francisco. This property was the site of the old Whipple Lumber Mill and the former town of Union Creek.

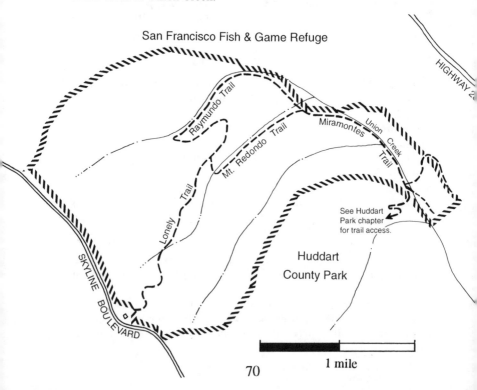

Henry Cowell Redwoods State Park

TO GET THERE. . . The southern unit is just south of Felton on Highway 9. The Fall Creek unit is just northwest of town on the Felton-Empire Road. The Rincon parking lot is 3.3 miles south of the main entrance on Highway 9.

This redwood-forested park is divided into 2 sizable units in the mountains near Felton.

Most visitors are unaware that the popular Redwood Grove and picnic area just south of Felton are only a small part of the park. The great bulk of the southern unit of this redwood preserve can be reached by well developed hiking trails from several roadside pullouts on Highway 9, from the park campground on Graham Hill Road, and from the picnic area near park headquarters (the day use entrance). This unit covers 1,737 acres and has about 15 miles of hiking trails.

If you think this park is all redwoods you will be surprised to find an amazing ecological variety, including oak, Ponderosa pine, chaparral, and knobcone pine habitat. Keep in mind, especially during the rainy season, that none of the trails that cross the San Lorenzo River have bridges.

The Redwood Grove Nature Trail Loop (near the picnic area) is the easiest and most popular trail in the park. It is less than 1 mile and is more of a stroll than a real hike, though it winds through one of the finest first-growth redwood groves south of San Francisco, and is especially pleasant on weekdays when the crowds are gone. Most of the redwoods in the rest of the park are second-growth.

Nearby is a 260-site picnic area, each with a picnic table, barbeque pit, and shared water supply.

This is a hilly park, and the vegetation corresponds to the area's geography. Lower areas are forested with redwood and riperian vegetation in places, and ridges and hilltops are covered with oak, madrone, digger pine, manzanita, and other chaparral plants. The distribution of plants is also connected to the availability of sunlight. Chaparral plants prefer the sunny ridgetops, while the understory plants of the redwood groves are satisfied with only indirect light and with occasional shafts of sunlight that penetrate the dense forest canopy.

A cross section of the park's ecology can be viewed on a short hike from the picnic area to the observation deck on the Ridge Trail, which climbs from the redwood-covered streambeds to the chaparral-covered ridgetops where a view of Santa Cruz and Monterey Bay are possible on clear days. The route is steep in places and there is little water along most of the trail, especially in summer. The trail, however, is only slightly more than 3 miles and is easily completed in 2 hours by most hikers. The

(Continued on page 74)

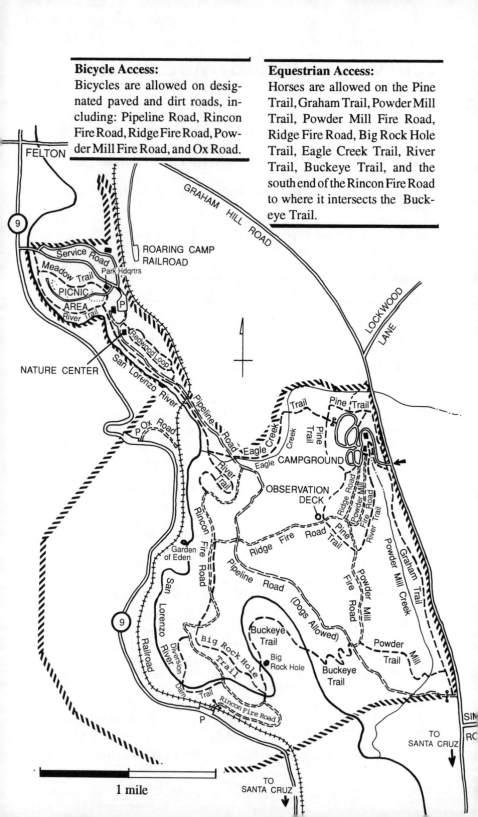

Bicycle Access:
Bicycles are allowed on designated paved and dirt roads, including: Pipeline Road, Rincon Fire Road, Ridge Fire Road, Powder Mill Fire Road, and Ox Road.

Equestrian Access:
Horses are allowed on the Pine Trail, Graham Trail, Powder Mill Trail, Powder Mill Fire Road, Ridge Fire Road, Big Rock Hole Trail, Eagle Creek Trail, River Trail, Buckeye Trail, and the south end of the Rincon Fire Road to where it intersects the Buckeye Trail.

FELTON

9

GRAHAM HILL ROAD

LOCKWOOD LANE

ROARING CAMP RAILROAD

Service Road

Meadow Trail

PICNIC AREA

Park Hdqrtrs

P

River Trail

NATURE CENTER

Redwood Loop

San Lorenzo River

Pipeline Road

Ox Road

P

Eagle Creek Trail

Eagle Creek

Pine Trail

Pine Trail

CAMPGROUND

River Trail

OBSERVATION DECK

Ridge Road

Powder Mill Fire Road

River Trail

Rincon Fire Road

Garden of Eden

Ridge Fire Road

Pine Trail

Pipeline Road (Dogs Allowed)

Powder Mill Fire Road

Graham Trail

Powder Mill Creek

San Lorenzo River

9

Railroad

Big Rock Hole Trail

Buckeye Trail

Big Rock Hole

Buckeye Trail

Powder Mill Trail

Diversion Dam Trail

Rincon Fire Road

P

TO SANTA CRUZ

TO SANTA CRUZ

SI RO

1 mile

Ohlone Day, held every October at Henry Cowell Redwoods State Park, is a hands-on celebration of Ohlone Indian culture and skills. You can learn how to make fire using a stick, how to chip arrowheads, or how to weave a water-tight basket using native materials. In this picture, two women use fire-heated rocks to cook acorn meal in a basket. For more information, call the Santa Cruz Mountains Natural History Association at (408)335-3174.

The Roaring Camp & Big Trees Railroad, adjacent to Henry Cowell Redwoods State Park, offers a ride through the redwoods on the steepest narrow-guage railroad grade in North America. For more information call (408)335-4484.

observation deck, on the water tank at the highest point of the trail, is a good place to relax and eat lunch.

Your leashed canine friend may accompany you on the 3-mile long paved Pipeline Road through the park.

There is a 112-unit year-around campground available on Graham Hill Road, complete with tables, fire rings, flush toilets, and hot showers. For reservations, call the park office at (408)335-4598.

See trail specifications on page 203

The mile-long Redwood Loop explores a beautiful old-growth redwood grove.

Fall Creek Unit

The Fall Creek unit is a steep, forested, and completely magnificent 2,335- acre park, tucked into a rugged canyon northwest of Felton. Start from the parking lot just off Felton-Empire Road and hike upstream. Where the north and south forks of Fall Creek meet,follow the South Fork Trail upstream to a flat area in a beautiful grove of maples, which becomes a brilliant blaze of color in autumn.

Most of this deep and shady canyon is occupied by second-growth redwoods, along with bay, big-leaf maple, and douglas fir. The forest floor is carpeted with sorrel, wild ginger, several kinds of ferns, and Solomon's seal, and chaparral grows on a few dry places.

Here the IXL Lime Company built 3 lime kilns in 1870, which were

Bicycle Access:
Bicycles are not permitted.

Equestrian Access:
Horses are allowed on all trails except where otherwise indicated on map.

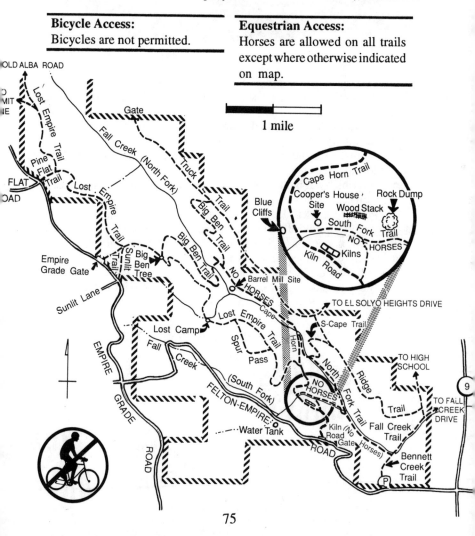

Explore the old lime kilns

fired with split redwood logs, some of which are still stacked across the creek from the kilns. By 1880 this was one of the state's most important lime producers. Above these deteriorated kilns rises Blue Cliff, an old limestone quarry.

From the kiln area hike the Cape Horn Trail to the North Fork Trail and follow the creek upstream to the scattered remains of a waterpowered barrel mill which was built in 1912. From here hike down-stream and back to the trailhead.

Fall Creek itself is one of the park's most wonderful features. It bounces wild and cold all summer, splashing over granite boulders which make it reminiscent of High Sierra streams. This beautiful canyon has more delightful qualities than I can mention here and is one of my favorite places in the Santa Cruz Mountains.

Bicycles and dogs are not allowed here. For more information, call park headquarters at (408) 335-4598.

See trail specifications on page 203

Hidden Villa Ranch

TO GET THERE ... take Highway 280 to the El Monte/Moody Road exit at Foothill College in Los Altos. The entrance is on Moody Road 2 . 5 miles from Highway 280 . Look for the "AYH" signs

This 1, 600 acre farm and wildland preserve is open to the public from Tuesday through Sunday from 9 a.m. until sundown. It is owned and maintained by the private nonprofit Trust for Hidden Villa.

An excellent trail system is maintained for use by equestrians and walkers, forming several easy to moderate loop routes through oak woodlands, chaparral, and grasslands. Bicycles are not allowed.

For more ambitious outings take the Ridge Trail into the Duveneck Windmill Pasture Area of Rancho San Antonio Open Space Preserve, or take the Black Mountain Trail 3 . 5 miles and 2, 300 feet up to the summit of Black Mountain in adjacent Monte Bello Open Space Preserve.

The Creek Trail follows Adobe Creek through a shady wooded

Equestrian Access:	**Bicycle Access:**
Horses are allowed on Creek Trail, Pipeline Trail, Grapeview Trail, Ridge Trail, and Black Mountain Trail.	Bicycles are not permitted.

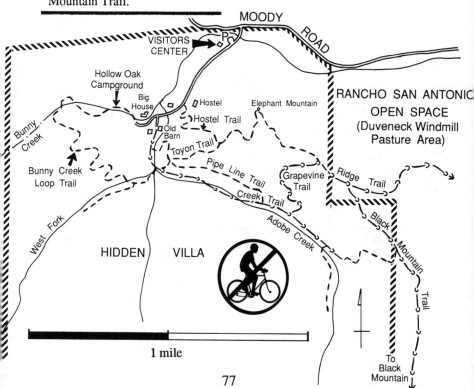

77

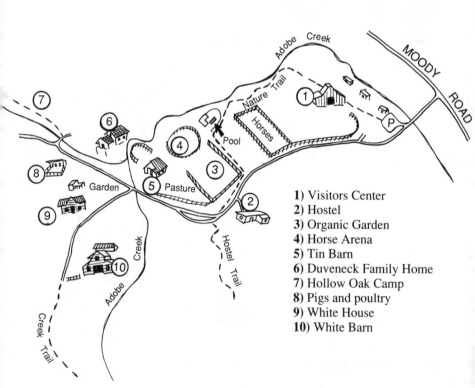

1) Visitors Center
2) Hostel
3) Organic Garden
4) Horse Arena
5) Tin Barn
6) Duveneck Family Home
7) Hollow Oak Camp
8) Pigs and poultry
9) White House
10) White Barn

canyon that makes a refreshing contrast to the exposed farm area on hot days.

The White House and White Barn are the oldest buildings on the property, constructed in the 1880's. Frank and Josephine Duveneck founded Hidden Villa in 1925 and added most of the other buildings, including the Duveneck family home, which was completed in 1930. You will also find a Visitors Center, Youth Hostel, organic garden, horse arena, tin barn for sheep and cows, Hollow Oak Camp, and pig and poultry facilities. This is an old fashioned working farm with lots of antique agricultural equipment on display.

The Hidden Villa Hostel is open from September 1 through May. It has group, family, and couples cabins, a large living room, and kitchen. Established in 1937, it is the oldest youth hostel west of the Hudson River. For more information call (415)949 8648.

Hidden Villa also has a summer camp program for kids from ages 7 through 16 years. Hiking, swimming, games, and farm chores are designed to foster multicultural understanding and environmental awareness. For more information, call (415)949-8641

Contributions are always needed to maintain the area and to keep all the programs growing. Send your tax deductible donations to : Hidden Villa, 26870 Moody Road, Los Altos Hills, CA 94022 .

For more information, call (415)948-4690.

Huddart County Park

TO GET THERE . . . take Woodside Road 3.5 miles west from Highway 280 and turn north on Kings Mountain Road.

This is one of San Mateo County's most popular parks, and its many recreational facilities often make it more crowded than most hikers like. Fortunately, however, you can leave the parking lots and picnic areas behind and explore about 15 miles of trails. The park covers 973 acres of oak woodlands, chaparral, Douglas fir and redwood forests.

This is a steep park, with trails to match. Easy walkers may want to take the .75 mile nature trail near the park entrance station. A more challenging route follows West Union Creek via Richard's Road Trail to near the Youth Group Camp, and then returns by way of the Service Road. A more ambitious loop around the park, climbing the 2,000 foot Skyline Ridge may be accomplished by continuing uphill on the Richard's Road Trail, turn left on the Skyline Trail, and left (downhill) on the Chinquapin Trail.

This route offers a cross section of Santa Cruz Mountains ecology.

1 mile

See trail specifications on page 203

Bicycle Access:
Bicycles are not permitted.

Equestrian Access:
Horses are allowed on all trails
except the Chickadee Trail and
the Redwood Trail.

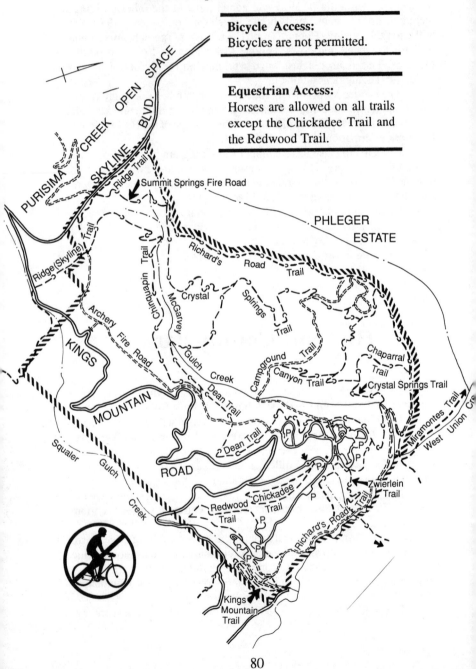

80

Oak woodlands cover the park's lower elevations, with chaparral on dry ridgetops and redwood groves are tucked into streambed furrows. Tanoak, madrone, bay, Douglas fir, and several species of oak also contribute to this plant kingdom hodgepodge. The park's animal inhabitants include Black-tail deer, squirrels, racoons, foxes, bobcats, woodrats, several species of lizards and snakes, and an abundant variety of birds.

You can visit the historic Woodside Store at the intersection of Kings Mountain Road and Tripp Road. It was built in 1853. The store is open Tuesdays, Thursdays, Saturdays, and Sundays from noon to 5 p.m. For information, call (415) 574-6441.

An understanding of the human history of the park is important for an appreciation of what you will see here. The redwood groves you see are second-growth descendants of an ancient forest of giants that was logged in the 1850's and 60's to supply the Bay Area's booming cities with lumber. You can still see massive stump remnants of the original forest and trace the "skid road" depressions up the hillsides, created by oxen dragging logs to the nearby sawmills.

This park has more than the usual recreational opportunties. A childrens' playground, picnicking and barbecuing facilities, and an archery range are provided, and an overnight campground is open in summer on a first-come, first-serve basis. Bicycles are not allowed.

There is an entry fee. For group picnic site reservations and other information, call (415) 363-4021 or (415)851-0326.

You can visit the historic Woodside Store at the intersection of Kings Mountain Road and Tripp Road. It was built in 1853.

Jasper Ridge Biological Preserve

HOW TO GET THERE . . . there are two entrances. To reach the Searsville Lake entrance take Sand Hill Road west from Highway 280. To reach the Escobar Gate entrance take Alpine Road west from Highway 280, turn right on Westridge Drive, and right on Escobar Road.

Jasper Ridge is famous for its spectacular springtime displays of wildflowers and remnants of native California grasslands. Operated by Stanford University, this preserve boasts examples of all of the plant communities found in the Santa Cruz Mountains.

The ridge's serpentine soils, lacking essential nutrients needed by most plants, allow native grasses to resist the invasion of alien annuals. Of the 16 grasses found on the serpentine, 12 are natives, including purple needle grass, pin bluegrass, and big squirreltail. This serpentine community, including the checkerspot butterfly, has been the object of much scientific study of ecology and population biology.

This 1,300-acre preserve is only accessible by docent escort. Guided walks are regularly scheduled and independent group tours may be arranged. Docent walks observe wildflowers, birds, geology, lichens, trees, grasses, and other areas of interest. For more information, call Stanford University at (415) 327-2277.

La Honda Creek Open Space Preserve

TO GET THERE. . . from Skyline Boulevard take Bear Gulch Road .6 miles west and turn left on Allen Road. The preserve entrance is at a metal gate that crosses the road 1.1 miles from Bear Gulch Road.
PLEASE NOTE: Because Allen Road is private, you must have a permit to enter this preserve. To obtain one, contact the Midpeninsula Regional Open Space District at (415) 691-1200. Because parking is not allowed outside the main gate, you will get the combination to the gate lock when you receive the permit.

The best thing about this preserve is the wonderful variety of scenery revealed by even a short and leisurely walk.

Gentle grassland slopes provide unobstructed mountain and ocean views to the south and west. Oak-madrone woodlands occupy the higher and drier zones, mixing easily with Douglas fir, and then blending quickly with second-growth redwood in the moist and shady canyon bottoms .

Even a 2-to-4 mile ramble will take you through all courses of this ecological smorgasbord, which combines to form bountiful wildlife habitat. Throughout the preserve you will hear a perpetual medley of bird songs: the rat-a-tat tapping of woodpeckers among the oaks, the strident caw of steller jays in the redwood groves, and the piercing call of red-tailed hawks circling high above the grasslands.

Signs of deer, bobcats, coyotes, and other mammals attest to this area's value to wildlife.

Springtime brings an exceptional number and variety of wildflowers. Pink filaree flowers carpet the grassy slopes, mixed with blue-eyed grass, checkerbloom, buttercup, lupine, poppies, and wild cucumber. I

83

was particularly impressed by the dense clusters of Douglas iris where grassland and oak woods meet.

As of this writing, parts of the main dirt road trail, near the power lines, are nearly impassable because of dense brush. Fortunately, this section can be easily avoided by taking cow trails across the grassland and reconnecting with the trail to the east. Adventurous trail users may want to explore the many old ranch and logging roads in various stages of disrepair.

Following the route on the map you will encounter a wooden fence near a water tank. This area has several residences and is closed to the public. All buildings and immediate vicinities are closed to the public.

This preserve is open from dawn to dusk.

Equestrian Access:
Horses are allowed.

Bicycle Access:
Bicycles are allowed.

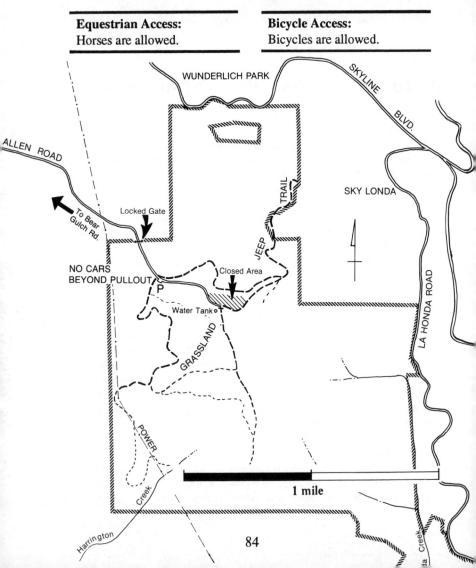

Loch Lomond Recreation Area

TO GET THERE... from Felton (on Highway 9) or from Scotts Valley (on Highway 17) take Mount Hermon Road, turn north on   Zayante Road and Lompico Road to Lompico. Turn left on West Drive and follow the signs to the recreation area.

Tucked into the forested Newell Creek watershed north of Felton, Loch Lomond is a beautiful setting for picnicking, walking, and fishing. Be aware, however, that the area may be closed during drought years.

This reservoir, the water supply for the city of Santa Cruz, has a boat launch ramp for private boats. Sailboats and gas-powered boats are not allowed. The recreation area also has beautifully maintained picnic areas with clean restrooms and barbeques.

Fishing is popular, especially for rainbow trout, bluegill, sunfish, and largemouth bass. The Department of Fish and game occasionally stocks the lake with trout. Swimming is not allowed.

The Shore Trail makes a gentle parallel along the reservoir, and connects with the Deer Flat Trail, which goes to the more remote areas.

The Big Trees Trail takes a 1 mile steep loop through second-growth redwoods, tanbark oak, and madrone. Despite its name, there are no really big trees.

The area was logged in the late 1800's and early 1900's and was purchased by the San Lorenzo Valley Water District in 1947. In 1959 the city of Santa Cruz bought the land and built the earthen dam that holds the 8,700 acre foot reservoir we enjoy today.

Under the supervision of the Water Department of the City of Santa Cruz, Loch Lomond is open March 1 through September 15 from sunrise to sunset. For more information, call the Santa Cruz Water Department at (408)335-7424.

Boating Regulations:
1) Gas motors are prohibited. Electric motors are allowed.
2) Canvas boats, plastic boats, styrofoam boats, and kayaks are not allowed.
3) Canoes must be at least 13 feet long and 32 inches wide.
4) Inflatables must be at least 6 feet long.
5) Boaters under 16 years must be accompanied by an adult.
6) Boaters must only leave or enter boats at docks provided.

Equestrian Access:
Horses are prohibited.

Bicycle Access:
Bicycles are prohibited.

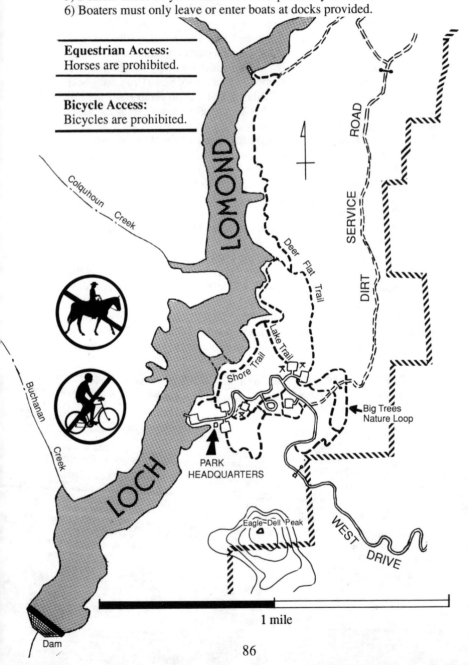

Colquhoun Creek

Buchanan Creek

LOMOND

LOCH

Deer Flat Trail

Lake Trail

Shore Trail

SERVICE ROAD

DIRT

Big Trees Nature Loop

PARK HEADQUARTERS

Eagle-Dell Peak

WEST DRIVE

1 mile

Dam

Long Ridge Open Space Preserve

TO GET THERE . . . park at the Grizzly Flat turnout on Skyline Boulevard, 3 miles south of Page Mill Road, and 3.5 miles north of Saratoga Gap (Skyline and Highway 9). The turnout is identified by a gate and wooden fence, and is near a "Palo Alto City Limit" sign.

Long Ridge is one of the most beautiful and walkable places in the Santa Cruz Mountains. It has spectacular ridgetop views, grassy hills, shady wooded canyons, and a delightful pond that makes a perfect place for lunch. Most of the trails are former ranch roads.

The southern part of this 1,217-acre preserve includes Hickory Oak Ridge, which is accessible from Skyline Boulevard at a metal gate 1.6 miles north of Highway 9. Parking is limited. Stately groves of oak, madrone, and Douglas fir crown this beautiful ridge, with sweeping views of the mountains and ocean an added attraction. On a very clear day I was able to see as far as the Farallon Islands. I have also found this to be a great place to look for signs of wildlife. A dirt road trail follows the ridge crest.

A beautiful pond lies on the boundary between the preserve and land owned by a Zen Buddhist retreat. The Buddhists are friendly and allow walkers to loop around the pond and back up the ridge. The trail going downstream from the pond forms part of an ideal loop walk downstream along Peters Creek and then uphill to the ridge top and then back to the pond. In the valley north of the pond along this route is an abandoned apple orchard that offers a welcome treat in the fall.

There is a logging road trail connecting this preserve with Portola State Park to the west, though as of this writing, the route is not marked.

Dog owners will be glad to know that their pets are allowed on leash at the grassy area at the Grizzly Flat entrance.

For more information contact the Midpeninsula Regional Open Space District at (415) 691-1200.

Equestrian Access:
All trails are open to horses, though the Peters Creek Loop may be closed seasonally after rain.

Bicycle Access:
All trails are open to bicycles, though Peters Creek Loop may be closed seasonally after rain.

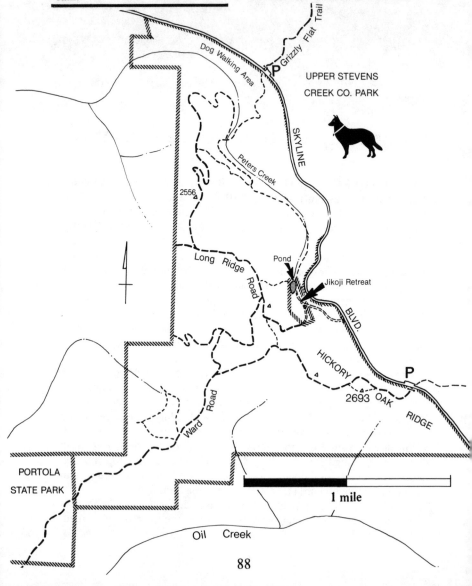

Off-Road Bicycling

Off-road bicyclists are the fastest growing group of trail users.
Because of complaints from other trail users, most public agencies limit bicycles to dirt road trails. Fortunately, many of the trails in the Santa Cruz Mountains were originally ranch, logging, and fire roads that are wide enough to accomodate bicycles without conflicting with the enjoyment of people who prefer slower means of transportation.

Midpeninsula Regional Open Space Preserves: *All trails are open to bicycle use except for those marked otherwise at trailheads.*
State Parks: *Bicycles are allowed on all fire roads unless otherwise posted*
Soquel Demonstration Forest: *Bicycles are allowed on all trails.*
Santa Clara County Parks: *Mountain bikes are allowed on designated trails in Stevens Creek, Upper Stevens Creek, and Santa Teresa county parks.*
San Mateo County Parks: *Off-road bicycles are permitted only on the following trails.*
• *Pescadero Creek County Park-Pomponio Road, Bridge Trail, Old Haul Road, Portola State Park Road.*
• *San Bruno Mountain County Park-Saddle Loop Trail, Day Camp Access Trail, Old Guadalupe Trail. Radio Road.*
• *Sawyer Camp Trail.*
• *San Pedro Valley County Park- Weiler Ranch Road.*
Golden Gate National Recreation *Area: Bicycles are allowed on fire roads on Sweeney Ridge.*

The Last Grizzly

Grizzly bears were once common in the Santa Cruz Mountains, feasting on berries and acorns, digging for roots, and gathering along streams to fish during the annual runs of salmon and steelhead. Their diet was nearly identical to that of the Ohlone Indians, who feared and revered the great bears.

But this was an abundant land, with a mild climate, and there was food enough for all. In fact, California probably had more grizzlies than anywhere else.

When the Spanish grazed cattle over their vast ranchos in the late eighteenth and early nineteenth centuries the opportunistic bears acquired a taste for beef.

This was a banquet that ended abruptly though, soon after California became a state in 1850. Gold, climate, and land brought hordes of immigrants to the Bay Area, including loggers and ranchers who claimed the Santa Cruz Mountains for their commercial value, leaving dwindling habitat for both grizzlies and Ohlone. The bears were shot on sight through the 1860's, 70's, and into the 1880's, when the last one was killed.

Around Bonny Doon Mountain lived an old sow bear who had acquired a taste for pork. Late one night in November of 1885 she made the mistake of carrying off a 300-pound hog that rancher Orrin Blodgett had been fattening for market. When Orrin found the remains that the bear had stashed away for later consumption he readied his rifle and waited. Several nights passed before the bear returned; and when she did, the rancher met up with her unexpectedly, with barely enough time to raise his muzzle-loaded rifle and fire—or at least that's his side of the story.

The dead bear weighed in at 642 pounds; the last grizzly ever reported in the Santa Cruz Mountains.

Los Trancos Open Space Preserve

TO GET THERE. . . take Page Mill Road 5 miles west from Highway 280. The parking lot is uphill from Foothill Park and about 1 mile east of Skyline Boulevard.

This 274- acre preserve, with about 5 miles of trails, offers several easy trail loops through grasslands, chaparral, and oak woods, with sweeping views of the bay, Mount Diablo, and San Francisco. Los Trancos straddles a revealing part of the 600 mile long San Andreas Fault, and displays many features that evidence fault activity. The trail passes Los Trancos Creek, which follows an old line of broken rock within the San Andreas fault zone. Posts mark the location of known fault fractures.

Sag ponds, pressure ridges, and terraces in the park were created by the buckling of the rock under pressure from fault movement. Near the parking lot you will find conglomerate rocks that were sheared from Loma Prieta, a mountain 25 miles to the south, and were transported here by the gradual movement of land along the fault. The earth's crust is divided into

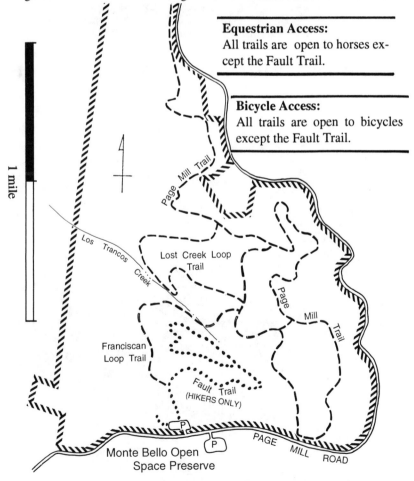

Equestrian Access:
All trails are open to horses except the Fault Trail.

Bicycle Access:
All trails are open to bicycles except the Fault Trail.

1 mile

Page Mill Trail

Los Trancos Creek

Lost Creek Loop Trail

Page Mill Trail

Franciscan Loop Trail

Fault Trail (HIKERS ONLY)

PAGE MILL ROAD

Monte Bello Open Space Preserve

massive plates of rock floating on the earth's mantle-- and this is where 2 of them scrape together. East of here is the North American Plate, and to the west is the Pacific Plate. Naturalist tours leave from the parking lot on Sundays, and they are well worth attending. For more information, call the Midpeninsula Regional Open Space District at (415)691-1200.

This is a brilliant wildflower gardens in April when iridescent fields of blue-eyed grass, poppies, buttercups, and many others form a flowery carpet. Madrone and bay trees are common here, as are black, blue, canyon live, and coast live oaks.

Los Trancos can be used as a starting point for exploring other open space preserves to the south, and you can even hike about 8 miles from here to Saratoga Gap, where the "Skyline-to-the-Sea" trail begins. This trans-park route can be started on Page Mill Road just downhill from the parking lot.

A short Guide to Earthquake Faults

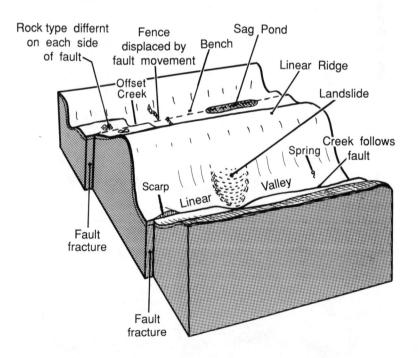

The Santa Cruz Mountains were formed and shaped by movement along the San Andreas and associated fault systems.

These mountains straddle the San Andreas Fault, which is where 2 vast continental plates are grinding together. The Pacific Plate extends from this fault westward to beyond the middle of the Pacific Ocean. The North American Plate begins at the fault and goes eastward to the middle of the Atlantic Ocean.

Earthquakes on this fault system are responsible for many of the land forms that you can learn to recognize.

This fence, at Los Trancos Open Space Preserve, was offset by movement on the San Andreas Fault.

This sag pond, at Monte Bello Open Space Preserve, was formed where a bend in the San Andreas Fault made a sagging gap that filled with water.

From the air you can clearly see that the Crystal Springs and San Andreas Reservoirs lie in a straight and narrow rift valley which was formed by the grinding of the continental plates along the San Andreas Fault.

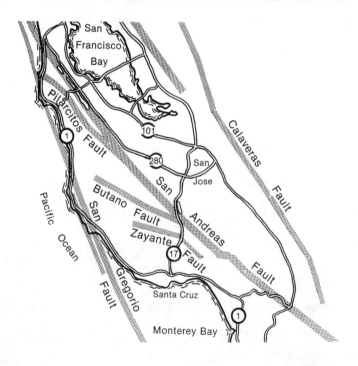

McNee Ranch State Park

TO GET THERE... take Highway 1 just north of Montara and park at the Martini Creek parking lot (8.1 miles north of Highway 92). Parking is across from a group of cypress trees. Walk carefully along the highway for a fifth of a mile to a white metal gate, where a dirt road enters the park.

This is one of the least known parks in the Santa Cruz Mountains, and it is in danger of being sliced in two by a proposed re-routing of Highway 1.

McNee Ranch sweeps down the steep slopes of Montara Mountain to just above the vertical cliffs of Devil's Slide. Views of the ocean and mountains are seen from the ranch roads that make up the trail system. The hills are covered mainly with coastal scrub.

Be aware that strong and cold Pacific winds and dense fog lash these exposed slopes. So be prepared for changing conditions even on calm sunny days.

McNee Ranch shares an eastern boundary with San Pedro Valley County Park and the San Francisco Fish and Game Refuge. You can take a trail one way 4.5 miles from the trailhead on Highway 1 to the parking lot at San Pedro Valley County Park. This is a vigorous route, with an elevation gain of more than 1,500 feet and a lot of commanding views of the ocean and mountains along the way.

The expedition of Spanish explorer Gaspar de Portola camped on the bank of Martini Creek on October 30, 1769, just prior to their discovery of San Francisco Bay.

Open from dawn to dusk, this park has none of the facilities you might expect at a state park. For more information, call the San Mateo Coast District of the California Department of Parks and Recreation at (415) 726-8800.

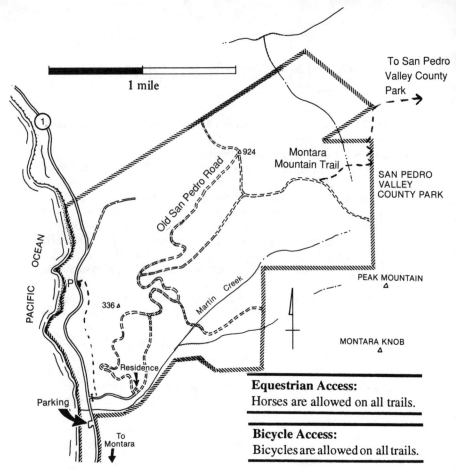

Equestrian Access:
Horses are allowed on all trails.

Bicycle Access:
Bicycles are allowed on all trails.

The Montara Hostel, 1.4 miles south of the park entrance, is a good and inexpensive place to spend the night. For information, call them at (415) 728-7177,

Point Montara Lighthouse Hostel overlooks the rugged coast south of McNee Ranch State Park.

Monte Bello Open Space Preserve

TO GET THERE . . . take Page Mill Road about 5 miles west from Highway 280 to the parking area just downhill from the Los Trancos parking lot.

Monte Bello is a large and varied land of deep wooded canyons, windswept grassy ridges, the San Andreas Fault, and a great system of trails.

With 13 miles of well-maintained trails, this 3,258-acre preserve is the hub of a lot of walking opportunities. Los Trancos Open Space is just across Page Mill Road; the Duveneck Windmill Pasture Area and Hidden Villa Ranch are reached by trail via the Black Mountain Trail; Saratoga Gap Open Space is just to the south, with trail connections to Skyline Ridge, Long Ridge, Russian Ridge and Coal Creek open space preserves. It's about 8 miles from Page Mill Road to Saratoga Gap (Skyline Boulevard/Highway 9 intersection); and from there another 28 miles to the ocean.

From the parking area on Page Mill (near the Los Trancos Open Space parking) take the 3-mile Stevens Creek Nature Trail, which descends into a wooded canyon and then climbs past gnarled old oaks and through an abandoned walnut orchard. Pick up a brochure for the self-guided walk at the parking area. Next to the Canyon Trail, which goes all the way to Saratoga Gap, is a marshy sag pond filled with cattails and other aquatic plants. This pond is right on a fracture of the San Andreas Fault, and was formed when the land dropped. Evidence of fault movement is common nearby, where the unstable ground is landsliding.

From the Page Mill Road parking area it is a 2-mile walk and a 840-foot ascent via the broad Indian Creek Trail to the scenic summit of Black

(Continues on page 99)

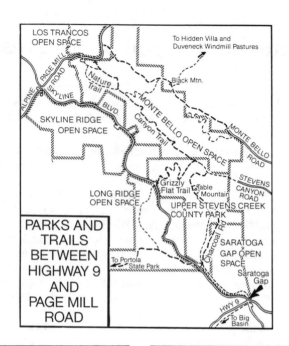

PARKS AND TRAILS BETWEEN HIGHWAY 9 AND PAGE MILL ROAD

LOS TRANCOS OPEN SPACE

To Hidden Villa and Duveneck Windmill Pastures

Black Mtn.

Nature Trail

SKYLINE

ALPINE

PAGE MILL ROAD

SKYLINE BLVD.

MONTE BELLO OPEN SPACE

Canyon Trail

SKYLINE RIDGE OPEN SPACE

MONTE BELLO ROAD

STEVENS CANYON ROAD

Grizzly Flat Trail

Table Mountain

LONG RIDGE OPEN SPACE

UPPER STEVENS CREEK COUNTY PARK

Charcoal Rd.

SARATOGA GAP OPEN SPACE

To Portola State Park

Saratoga Gap

HWY 9

To Big Basin

Equestrian Access:
All trails are open to horses except the Stevens Creek Nature Trail.

Bicycle Access:
All trails are open to bicycles except the Stevens Creek Nature Trail.

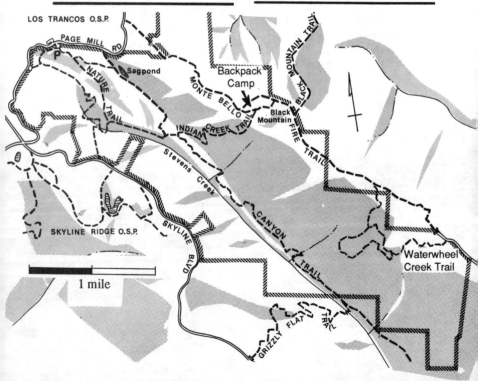

LOS TRANCOS O.S.P.

PAGE MILL RD.

Sagpond

NATURE TRAIL

MONTE BELLO TRAIL

INDIAN CREEK TRAIL

Backpack Camp

BLACK MOUNTAIN TRAIL

Black Mountain

BLACK MOUNTAIN FIRE TRAIL

Stevens Creek

SKYLINE RIDGE O.S.P.

SKYLINE BLVD.

CANYON TRAIL

Waterwheel Creek Trail

GRIZZLY FLAT TRAIL

1 mile

(Continued from page 97)

Mountain. With little shade along the way, this is not an easy walk at midday when it's hot. From Black Mountain there is a 3-mile downhill trail to Duveneck Windmill Pasture Area and on to Hidden Villa Ranch.

Just west of Black Mountain is the Black Mountain Backpack Camp. What a place to sleep: coyote serenades, with owl counterpoint melodies; and the whole urban spectacle sprawled out below. Camping here is by permit only and open flres are prohibited. Camp stoves are allowed. For permits and information, call the open space office.

Perhaps eventually there will be better public access to the other end of the preserve at the uphill end of Monte Bello Road, via Stevens Canyon Road from Cupertino. This area has excellent trails and some of the most striking views in the Santa Cruz Mountains. Docent tours for 5 to 25 people can be scheduled by calling the open space district office. This 3.5-mile guided walk is jammed with scenery and history.

You may want to stop at one of several wineries just down Monte Bello Road on your way back.

The habitat diversity of this land makes it perfect for lots of wildlife, including bobcats, coyotes, deer, raccoons, and a wide variety of birds. Even mountain lions are known to patrol this region.

Call the Midpeninsula Regional Open Space District at (415) 691-1200 for information on guided walks through this park.

Mount Madonna County Park

TO GET THERE...take Hecker Pass Highway (Route 152) west from Gilroy.

This is a park for people who like scenic diversity, panoramic vistas, and steep trails. The park has more than 17 miles of foot and bridle trails which explore peaceful groves of redwood and oak, snake through scratchy expanses of chaparral, and gallop across open grassy hills. The park has 3,093 acres and plenty of room for even the most undauntable of hikers. To further tax your energy, it straddles a ridgetop and few of the trails come anywhere close to being level.

One of the steepest trails goes to Sprig Lake, a small but deep reservoir open to fishing by visitors between the ages of 5 and 12.

The Merry-Go-Round Trail is a steep and scenic whirlwind tour of all the park's ecological communities. It is especially pleasant in early spring when the grassy areas at the lower elevations turn green and are splashed with flowery colors. A 5-mile loop can be made by combining the Miller, Loop, Merry-Go-Round, Contour, and Ridge trails. Begin the hike just past park headquarters at the end of the road.

(Continues on page 101)

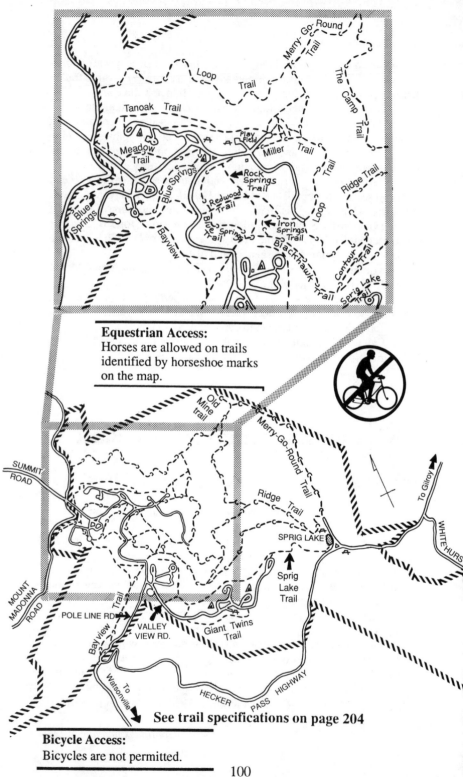

Equestrian Access:
Horses are allowed on trails identified by horseshoe marks on the map.

See trail specifications on page 204

Bicycle Access:
Bicycles are not permitted.

100

(Continued from page 99)

This land once belonged to cattle baron Henry Miller, who used it as a summer headquarters. Most of the buildings were removed after his death in 1916 and now only the foundation remains. The rare, white fallow deer may be seen in a penned area.

Picnicking and camping facilities are available on a first-come, first-served basis. For information, call park headquarters at (408) 842-2341.

Pescadero Creek County Park

TO GET THERE... It is accessible by trail from San Mateo Memorial and Sam McDonald county parks and Portola State Park; or by driving Alpine Road and heading south (downhill) on Camp Pomponio Road to the Tarwater Trail parking lot.

This is a large forested park on the watershed of one of the Santa Cruz Mountains' major creeks. For years this 6,000-acre park was used largely for reaching adjoining parks; but now there are two trail camps which make Pescadero a major target for backpackers. From Sam McDonald County Park, Tarwater Flat Trailcamp is 5 miles, and Shaw Flat Trailcamp is 4 miles. For reservations, call (415) 363-4021 or (415)879-0212.

The Old Haul Road Trail connects San Mateo County Memorial Park and Portola State Park by passing through Pescadero Creek County Park. This approximately 6- mile trail from Memorial Park can be started at the swimming area by the dam on Pescadero Creek. Follow Pescadero Creek Trail east to Wurr Road at the bridge and turn right, continuing the route south a short distance to a small wooden bridge on the left side of the road. This trail has an easy grade.

(Continues on page 104)

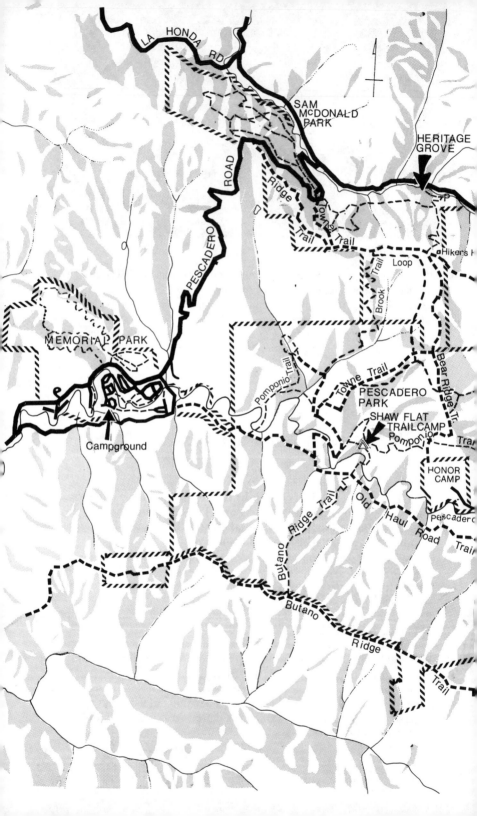

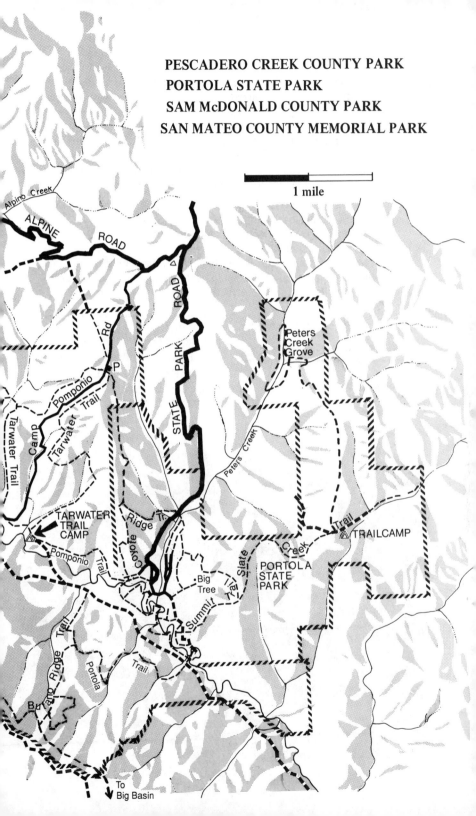

PESCADERO CREEK COUNTY PARK
PORTOLA STATE PARK
SAM McDONALD COUNTY PARK
SAN MATEO COUNTY MEMORIAL PARK

1 mile

(Continued from page 101)

Pescadero Creek County Park was heavily logged earlier in this century and today has few virgin redwoods, and evidence of logging is still visible. Rusting logging cables can still be found wrapped around redwood trunks and notches for loggers' springboards can still be found on old redwood stumps. It has been estimated that the Santa Cruz Mountains have yielded more than 10 billion feet of lumber since the Gold Rush. This land was acquired by the county to be dammed and flooded by a reservoir. When the plan was abandoned the land became a park.

Old Haul Road Trail (5.7 miles): The main artery through the park. A popular bicycle route, it intersects many other trails.

Pomponio Trail (5.3 miles): Traverses the park and connects with many trails and both trail camps.

Tarwater Loop Trail (4.7 miles): From the trailhead on Camp Pomponio Road, this pleasant and ecologically diverse loop combines old logging roads with new trail construction.

Equestrian Access:
Horses are allowed on all trails.

SEE MAP ON PAGE 102

Bicycle Access:
Bicycles are only allowed on The Old Haul Road, the Ridge Trail, Camp Pomponio road, and the Portola State Park Road.

104

Pescadero Marsh Preserve

TO GET THERE ... take Highway I to Pescadero Road, just west of the town of Pescadero. There are parking accesses on Highway I at Pescadero State Beach and on Pescadero Road.

Pescadero Creek and Butano Creek flow together to form the largest coastal marsh between Monterey Bay and the Golden Gate. The short trails that run along the 640 acres of wetlands, provide bountiful opportunities for seeing such birds as least and spotted sandpipers, godwits, great egrets, herons, and migrating waterfowl. Several short trails offer birding opportunities among the preserve's cattails, tules, and willows. Great blue herons nest in the eucalyptus trees on the hill.

Late fall through early spring is the best time to see many of the more than 160 species of birds sighted here. For more information, call (415) 726-6238.

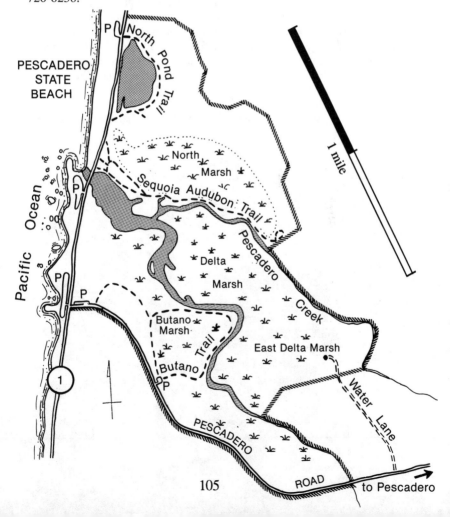

Picchetti Ranch Open Space Preserve

TO GET THERE . . . from Highway 280 take Foothill Expressway and Stevens Canyon Road south and turn west on Monte Bello Road.

This 372-acre preserve offers a leisurely walk through the late nineteenth century and an easy blend of natural and agrarian qualities.

There are only about 2 miles of trails here, and all are broad and of easy grade. You can walk through orchards of apricots, plums, walnuts, and pears to the small pond, where waterfowl gather in winter. In spring the fruit trees and wildflowers blossom and apricots may be eaten in early summer. Look for wild roses along this trail.

Heading north from the pond area the trails make an ascent to an oakwooded hilltop overlook of Stevens Creek Reservoir and the Santa Clara Valley.

This preserve is named for the Italian immigrants Vincenzo and Secondo Picchetti, who built the original homestead house in 1882. The large yellow ranch house was built in 1886, and the brick winery was added in 1896. It operated under the Picchetti Brothers label until 1963. After 20 years of disrepair, these buildings, which are listed in in the National Register of Historic Places, have been restored by the Midpeninsula Regional Open Space District and Sunrise Winery, which leases the buildings.

Sunrise Winery is open to the public Friday, Saturday, and Sunday from 11 a.m. to 3 p.m.

Though a separate piece of property, this preserve is administered as part of Monte Bello Open SpacePreserve. For more information call the Midpeninsula Regional Open Space District at (415) 691-1200.

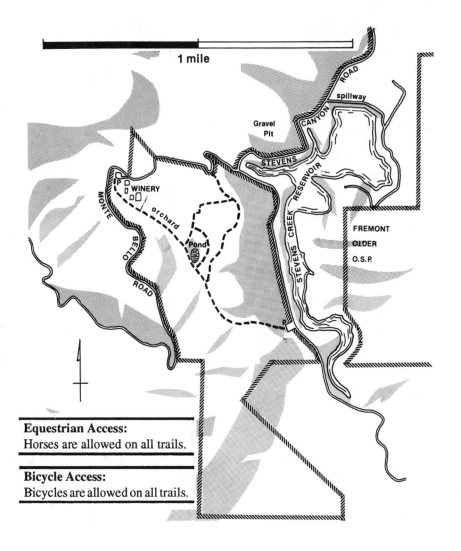

Equestrian Access:
Horses are allowed on all trails.

Bicycle Access:
Bicycles are allowed on all trails.

Pogonip Open Space Preserve

TO GET THERE... The east (downhill) access is from a pullout on Highway 9 about a mile north of Highway 1. To reach the University of California, Santa Cruz access take Bay Drive north from Highway 1 and continue north on Glenn Coolidge Drive to the service road and gate on the right side.

The city of Santa Cruz owns this preserve located between the

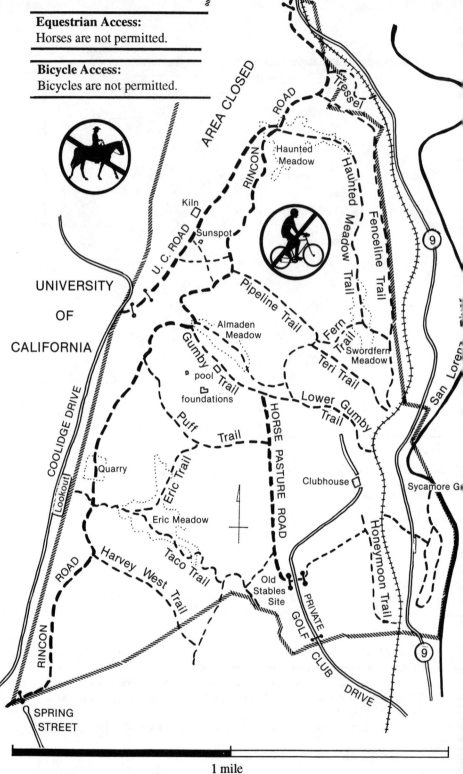

Equestrian Access:
Horses are not permitted.

Bicycle Access:
Bicycles are not permitted.

UNIVERSITY

OF

CALIFORNIA

AREA CLOSED

Tressel

RINCON ROAD

Haunted Meadow

U. C. ROAD

Kiln

Sunspot

Haunted Meadow Trail

Fenceline Trail

9

Pipeline Trail

Almaden Meadow

Fern Trail

Swordfern Meadow

Gumby Trail

pool

foundations

Teri Trail

Lower Gumby Trail

Puff Trail

HORSE PASTURE ROAD

San Lorenzo

Quarry

Eric Trail

Clubhouse

Sycamore G

COOLIDGE DRIVE

Lookout

Eric Meadow

Taco Trail

Honeymoon Trail

RINCON ROAD

Harvey West Trail

Old Stables Site

GOLF CLUB DRIVE

PRIVATE

9

SPRING STREET

1 mile

University of California and Henry Cowell Redwoods State Park. It is open from sunrise until 7 p.m. from April 1 through October 31 and from sunrise until 4 p.m. from November 1 through March 31. This is strictly a place for foot travel. Horses and bicycles are prohibited.

Pogonip has a good variety of habitat, including oak forests, second-growth redwood, grasslands,chaparral, and a sycamore grove along the San Lorenzo River. Some of the trails are steep, but the entire elevation range in the preserve is only 450 feet.

For a scenic 2 . 5 mile loop that includes a variety of habitats and a look at some old historic structures, park on the Coolidge Drive access and head downhill on U.C. Road and combine the Haunted Meadow Trail, the Fern Trail, the Gumby Trail, and the Rincon Road into a loop.

In 1849 Albion Jordan and Isaac Davis purchased 160 acres of this land to produce lime, used for making cement, from the area's plentiful limestone. Their lime kilns are still found on the U.C. Road above Sunspot Meadow. Jordan and Davis were so successful they purchased a wharf and schooners to ship lime to San Francisco.

In 1865 Henry Cowell purchased Jordan ' s interests in the company and in 1888 Cowell bought out Davis' interests. Competition from other lime producers forced the closure of the company in 1946. The city of Santa Cruz purchased the property from the Cowell Foundation in 1989.

In 1911 Fred Swanton built a golf course and stately clubhouse now called the Pogonip Club. The clubhouse and road are under lease to the Pogonip Club and are private. There is no public access.

For more information, call the city of Santa Cruz Parks & Recreation Department at (408)429-3777.

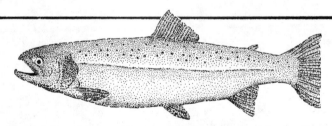

The San Lorenzo River is the largest stream in the Santa Cruz Mountains and it has the largest winter runs of steelhead trout and silver salmon south of San Francisco Bay.

The catch limit is two steelhead or salmon, or a combination. A current California fishing license is required. Fishing is restricted to the winter season only.

Steelhead trout make several runs up the river from the ocean in their lifetimes while salmon die after spawning once. Keep in mind that by throwing back a single adult female salmon to continue her spawning mission you may be responsible for contributing as many as 4,000 fish to the river.

Portola State Park

TO GET THERE...take Alpine Road west from Skyline Boulevard and turn south on Portola State Park Road.

Since 1945 Bay Area hikers have been exploring this redwood-forested park along Pescadero Creek. Its 2,800 acres offer more than 18 miles of trails through mostly second-growth redwood groves, though a few stands of big trees somehow survived. The park also offers excellent opportunities for picnicking, car camping, and trail camping.

The park's self-guided nature loop trail, which can be started just behind park headquarters, is a good place to start hiking. Though it's less than a mile long, the Sequoia Trail can be connected with the Iverson Trail for a more extensive hike. .

From here you can explore the Iverson Trail along Pescadero Creek, which contains water all year and has a wading pool near the visitors center. A 6 mile public trail (actually a fire road) connects Portola State Park with San Mateo County Memorial Park. The trail goes through Pescadero Creek County Park and can be reached from the Iverson Trail where it intersects a fire road southeast of Iverson Creek. This route begins beside the site of Iverson Cabin, built in 1860, and continues uphill to its intersection with the fire road to San Mateo Memorial and Sam McDonald parks. Bicycles are permitted on the Old Haul Road.

The Summit and Slate Creek trails can be combined to form an enjoyable hike of about 8.5 miles. The Summit Trail can be reached from

the Old Tree Trail which begins across the road from the Point Group Camp Area. This route goes to Slate Creek, Page Mill Site, and to the magnificent Peters Creek Grove. Before reaching the Page Mill Site there is a trailcamp about 3 miles from the trailhead at the intersection of Slate Creek Trail and Old Page Mill Road. The trailcamp has no water.

The trail beyond the Page Mill Site intersects unpaved Ward Road, which climbs through Long Ridge Open Space Preserve to the east to Skyline Boulevard, a distance of about 8 miles.

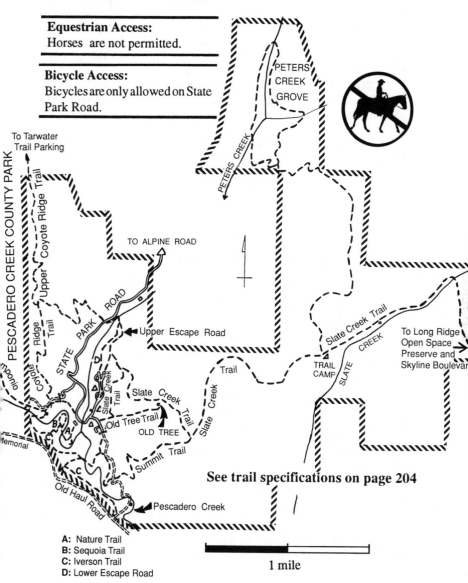

Equestrian Access:
Horses are not permitted.

Bicycle Access:
Bicycles are only allowed on State Park Road.

To Tarwater Trail Parking

PESCADERO CREEK COUNTY PARK

Upper Coyote Ridge Trail

PETERS CREEK GROVE

PETERS CREEK

TO ALPINE ROAD

Coyote Ridge Trail

STATE PARK ROAD

Upper Escape Road

Trail

Slate Creek Trail

SLATE CREEK

Slate Creek Trail

TRAIL CAMP

To Long Ridge Open Space Preserve and Skyline Boulevard

mpoio

Slate Creek Trail

Slate Creek Trail

Slate Creek

Old Tree Trail

OLD TREE

Summit Trail

See trail specifications on page 204

Memorial

Old Haul Road

Pescadero Creek

A: Nature Trail
B: Sequoia Trail
C: Iverson Trail
D: Lower Escape Road

1 mile

111

This park has 52 drive-up and 7 walk-in campsites, 4 group camps, 3 for 50 people and 1 for 25 people. Two nearby county parks, Pescadero Creek and Sam McDonald have accessible trailcamps.

Peters Creek Grove

Acquired by the Save the Redwoods League, the Peters Creek Grove is one of the most beautiful old-growth groves of redwoods in the Santa Cruz Mountains.

It has many large trees in a pristine environment; a kind of Shangri-La isolated from the outside world by a fairly strenuous 13-mile, round-trip hike. The trail is narrow and steep in places, but you will be amply rewarded by one of the most unspoiled places in the Bay Area.

To get there, take the Upper Escape Road or the Summit Trail to the Slate Creek Trail to the trail camp. Take the old jeep trail north, over an oak-forested ridge, and then take the footpath into the Peters Creek canyon.

Campsites may be reserved through MISTIX at 1(800) 444-7275. For park information, call (415) 948-9098.

Portola Valley Trails

Coal Mine Ridge

TO GET THERE... From Highway 280 exit at Alpine Road and head south. Park on the north side of Alpine Road near the Willowbrook Drive intersection.

Just east of the San Andreas Fault, this land is a pleasant patchwork of woodlands and grassy meadows. It is particularly enticing in late winter and early spring when the grasses are green and the wildflowers are in bloom. White oak, live oak, Douglas fir, and bay are abundant.

For a moderate 3.75-mile loop, combine the Old Spanish Trail, Coal Mine Trail, and Toyon Trail. You will enjoy views of Mount Diablo, Mount Tamalpais, and especially nearby Windy Hill.

These gently wooded 250 acres in the eastern foothills of the Santa Cruz Mountains are owned by the Portola Valley Ranch Homeowner's Association. Remember that the ridge is private land; so be sure to stay on the trails. Dogs and bicycles are not allowed.

For more information call the Portola Valley town hall at (415)851-1700.

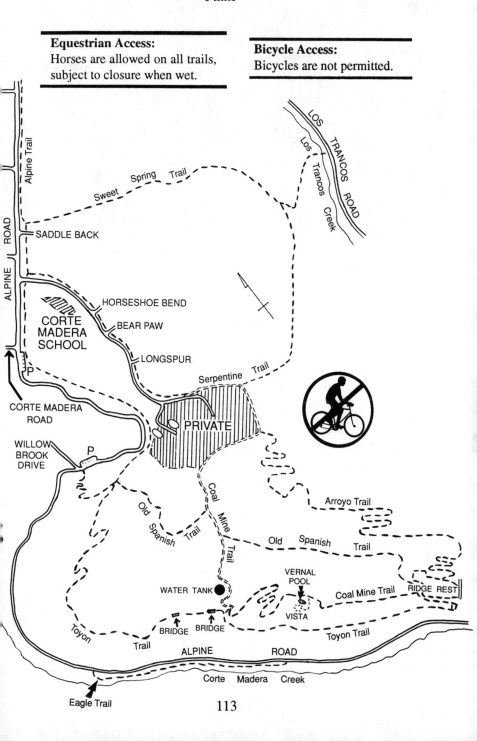

1 mile

Equestrian Access:
Horses are allowed on all trails, subject to closure when wet.

Bicycle Access:
Bicycles are not permitted.

LOS TRANCOS ROAD

Los Trancos Creek

Alpine Trail

Sweet Spring Trail

ALPINE ROAD

SADDLE BACK

HORSESHOE BEND

CORTE MADERA SCHOOL

BEAR PAW

LONGSPUR

P

Serpentine Trail

CORTE MADERA ROAD

WILLOW BROOK DRIVE

P

PRIVATE

Coal Mine Trail

Arroyo Trail

Old Spanish Trail

Old Spanish Trail

WATER TANK

VERNAL POOL

VISTA

Coal Mine Trail

RIDGE REST

Toyon Trail

BRIDGE BRIDGE

Toyon Trail

ALPINE ROAD

Corte Madera Creek

Eagle Trail

113

Coal Mine Ridge has a gentle and clearly marked trail system.

Larry Lane Trail

TO GET THERE... Park at the intersection of Portola Road and Hayfield Road in Portola Valley.

This is an easy 1.75-mile ramble through a wooded residential area to a grassy meadow where hay was once grown. You will ascend 500 feet, passing expensive homes and woodlands of oak, madrone, and bay.

Named for a local equestrian, this trail is for hikers and horses; bicycles are prohibited. There are rest benches along the way.

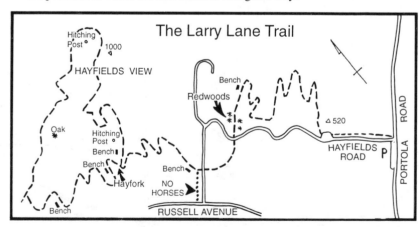

Pulgas Ridge Open Space

TO GET THERE. . . from Interstate 280 take Edgewood Road east, turn left on Crestview Road, and left on Edmonds Road. Park across from Redwood Center on Edmonds Road and walk up Hassler Road to a gate which marks the preserve boundary.

    This 293-acre preserve covers a ridge and 2 wooded valleys in the dry eastern foothills of the Santa Cruz Mountains. On the site of the former Hassler Health Home, a tuberculosis sanitarium which operated here from 1926 to 1972, the land is now in the process of reverting to a more natural condition. Relics of its former use still abound, though, with abandoned fire hydrants and steps that go nowhere. The preserve is named for the Pulgas Ridge on which it lies. The Pulgas Water Tunnel bisects the northern part of the preserve. Pulgas means "fleas" in Spanish.

    The hills are covered mainly with a combination of oak groves,

Equestrian Access:	**Bicycle Access:**
Horses are allowed on all trails.	Bicycles are allowed on all trails.

1 mile

chaparral, and grasslands. There are also a variety of ornamental trees and shrubs, especially around the site of the sanitarium, that seem to have adapted to our summer drought cycle.

There is only one real trail in this preserve, which makes a gentle ascent up the ridge and can be combined with the old Hassler Road to form an easy 3-mile loop with an elevation gain of about 400 feet. Because the section of Hassler Road between Redwood Center and the gate is private, be sure to stay on the authorized trail.

For more information, contact the Midpeninsula Regional Open Space District at (415) 691-1200.

Purisima Creek Redwoods Open Space Preserve

TO GET THERE... It's on Skyline Boulevard, 4.5 miles south of Highway 92. The parking lot is about 200 feet south of the Kings Mountain Store. The south entrance on Highway 1, at the east end of the Purisima Creek Road Trail, is about half a mile north of Kings Mountain Road on Skyline Boulevard. From Highway 1, just south of Half Moon Bay, the preserve's western access may be reached by taking Higgins-Purisima Road 4.5 miles to an entrance gate by a small bridge.

Climbing 1600 feet of steep terrain just east of Skyline Boulevard, this preserve has the northernmost major redwood forest in the Santa Cruz Mountains.

This 2,509-acre preserve also is wooded with Douglas fir, madrone, chaparral, and has lots of ridgetop views of the Pacific and the local mountains. Be prepared for a workout on about 17 miles of mostly steep trails.

Purisima Canyon is a major east-west drainage, with a perennial creek. Though the area was logged intensively between the 1850's and 1920, supporting 7 sawmills for awhile, the second-growth forest now rises tall, and stumps up to 16 feet in diameter remind us of the great trees that were cut.

There are still some majestic stands of large, first-growth redwoods in the park, however, though you won't find them along the park's main trails, which were built as logging roads.

For a spectacular, though physically-demanding 6-mile loop through Whittemore Gulch, combine the Whittemore Gulch Trail and the Harkins Fire Trail. This route involves an elevation range of about 1,400 feet.

(Continued on page 118)

116

Equestrian Access:
Horses are allowed on all trails except the Soda Gulch Trail and the footpath from the northern Skyline Boulevard parking lot.

Bicycle Access:
Bicycles are allowed on all trails except the Soda Gulch Trail and the footpath from the northern Skyline Boulevard parking lot.

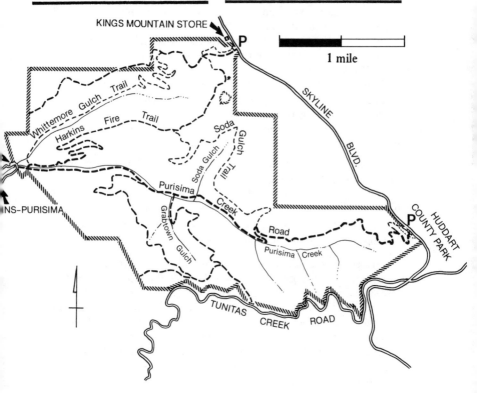

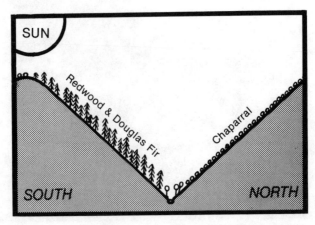

Notice how the vegetation differs dramatically between the shady north-facing and the sunny south-facing slopes.

A special trail for the physically handicapped has been built just off Skyline Boulevard north of Kings Mountain Road near where Purisima Creek Road intersects Skyline Boulevard.

The Soda Gulch Trail connects the Harkins Fire Trail with the Purisima Creek Trail. Passing mostly through second-growth redwoods, it is a fairly gentle route that is open to foot travel only. These 3 trails form a strenuous 10-mile loop from the Purisima Creek Road entrance on Skyline Boulevard.

The Purisima Creek Trail is an old logging road that connects Skyline Boulevard with Higgins-Purisima Road. This route is 4.2 miles one way, with an elevation range of 1600 feet.

Unfortunately, this route requires backtracking, unless you arrange car shuttles between the upper and lower ends of your trek.

For a spectacular, though physically-demanding 6-mile loop through Whittemore Gulch, combine the Whittemore Gulch Trail and the Harkins Fire Trail. This route requires an elevation range of about 1,400 feet. The Harkins Fire Trail is quite steep in places.

The Grabtown Gulch Trail loop, from Tunitas Creek Road, is a 4-mile loop with an elevation range of 1200 feet.

This preserve provides an essential link in the proposed "City-to-theSea" trail, which begins at Edgewood County Park in Redwood City, follows the Crystal Springs Trail to Huddart Park, climbs to Skyline, and then continues down through Purisima Canyon to Higgins-Purisima Road. All of the trails needed for this crossing of the Santa Cruz Mountains already exist. It is ideal for equestrians as well as walkers

Being on the coast side of Skyline, be prepared for windy and foggy weather. For more information, call the Midpeninsula Regional Open Space District at (415) 691-1200.

The Fog Forest

The mountains of the eastern side of the Santa Cruz Mountains look dry and dusty, in a kind of hibernation, during the long summer drought season. But this is not the case in the Purisima Creek watershed, especially near the Skyline Boulevard area. Even during the driest part of summer luxuriant gardens of moss, and other green and growing plants fill the lush forest.

Many times I have walked this preserve, especially in the early morning, when the fog drifts heavily through the groves, condensing on the needles of redwood and Douglas fir trees and dripping to the ground as steady as a winter rain. This phenomena is called "fog drip" and it contributes a large share of this area's precipitation, in many places the equivalent of 20 or more inches of rain each year.

Warm air can hold more water vapor than cool air. Fog forms when an air mass cools and the water vapor condenses into water droplets that are small and light enough to stay suspended in the air.

Along the northern California coast are currents that draw deep and cold water to the ocean surface. When the moist marine winds approach the coast they are suddenly cooled by contact with this cold upwelling water and the moisture in the air condenses into fog.

You will notice that the fog is thickest at night and early morning, often burning off by mid day. This is because the temperature is lowest at

119

night, causing the water vapor to precipate into fog. As the temperature rises during the day, the air is able to absorb this fog.

When the Central Valley bakes during the summer months the hot inland air rises and sucks cool marine air in from the coast. This heavy moist air mass then sweeps over low areas such as San Francisco, but it usually can't quite make it over the Skyline Ridge area, stalling atop the ridge and delivering this vitalizing fog bath.

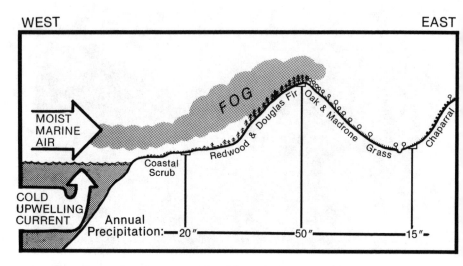

As moist marine air sweeps inland from the ocean it is forced upward by the Santa Cruz Mountains. As the air rises, it is cooled, causing water vapor to condense into fog and rain. This is why verdant forests thrive on the western slopes of the range.

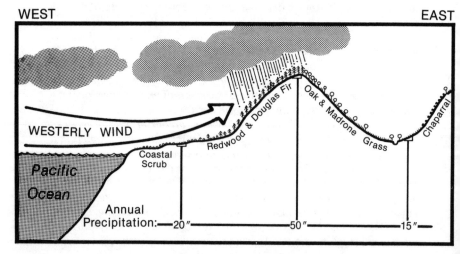

Quail Hollow Ranch County Park

TO GET THERE... from Highway 9 (north of Felton) take Glen Arbor Road and Quail Hollow Road west. The ranch is on the north side of quail Hollow Road.

There are few places in the Santa Cruz Mountains that manage to cram as much history, geology, and botany into such a small area as at Quail Hollow Ranch.

Be aware that this park is only open weekends and holidays, 10 a.m. to 4 p.m. from May to October.

Owned by Santa Cruz County, this 300-acre park features a beautiful forest of ponderosa pines, a tree that is common in the Sierra, but a rare relic of a cooler and moister time in the coastal ranges. This stately tree can be easily identified by needles about 10 inches long grouped in bunches of 3.

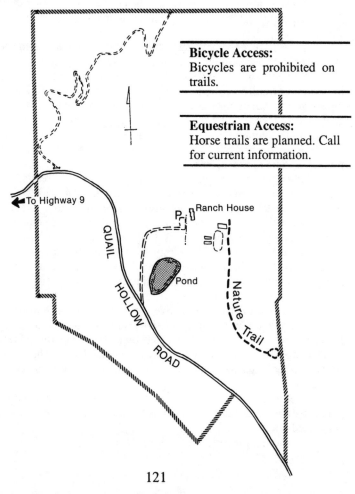

Bicycle Access:
Bicycles are prohibited on trails.

Equestrian Access:
Horse trails are planned. Call for current information.

To Highway 9

QUAIL HOLLOW ROAD

Ranch House

Pond

Nature Trail

Notice that this tree grows in the granitic sandy soils that are characteristic of this park. They were formed as an inland marine sand deposit 10-25 million years ago when this area was below the ocean near the rapidly uplifting California coast. Called the "Santa Margarita Formation", it lies on top of an impermeable layer of shale, forming the Santa Margarita Aquifer, which is an important source of groundwater for the San Lorenzo Valley.

This unusual geology makes this habitat for 2 endangered species: the silver-leaved manzanita, and the Ben Lomond wallflower.

You will notice that some of the ponderosa pines are riddled with thousands of small holes made by colonies of acorn woodpeckers to store the acorns they have gathered in the fall for later consumption. These lively birds, easily identified by their black and white markings and red head patch, live in colonies that defend an established territory and collectively share the feeding and raising of young. One popular "granary tree" is the ponderosa next to the ranch house.

Other biotic communities in this ranch include second-growth redwood, including mature dwarf redwoods that grow only 18-20 feet high in areas of shallow rocky soil; oak groves; chaparral; stream vegetation; and a pleasant little pond which is home to sunfish and largemouth bass, and a feeding place for blue herons, kingfishers, and other birds.

Because of the fragile ecology, visitors are encouraged to stay on the trail. As of this writing the only established footpath is a .5 mile long self guided nature trail, which passes through a grassy meadow and by stands of oak and ponderosa pine.

Joe Kenville and his family lived in the ranch house from the 1880's until it was sold to Emil Grunig in 1910. From 1937 until 1957 Lawrence Lane, the publisher of Sunset Magazine, owned the property and featured it in the magazine as an example of western ranch living. The laboratory lane put in for magazine related experiments can still be seen in the main ranch house.

The land was ranched by several other owners until the county purchased it in 1985. Legend maintains that the upstairs of the ranch house is haunted.

For more information, call (408)335 9348.

Rancho San Antonio Open Space Preserve & County Park

TO GET THERE... from Highway 280 take Foothill Boulevard south and turn west on Cristo Rey Drive Parking is in the adjacent Rancho San Antonio County Park.

With easy access to the Mountain View, Los Altos, and Cupertino vicinity, this is the most popular of the open space preserves. It's a perfect destination for walking, running, and picnicking. A well-established system of gentle trails will take you throughout the nearly 970 acres of this preserve.

Historic Deer Hollow Farm is one of the park's most popular features and is used for a variety of environmental education programs by the city of Mountain View, which leases the farm. For more information, call (415) 966-6331. It is especially popular with children. These old nineteenth-century farm buildings were built by the Grant brothers, who purchased the land in 1860 for cattle ranching. It is only about a mile from the parking lot via an easy and nearly level trail.

Rancho San Antonio was the name of this area when it was part of a Mexican land grant in the early nineteenth century.

This preserve is in the foothills on the east side of the range. With an elevation ranging from 400 to over 1,400 feet, this area is characterized by chaparral and grasslands and by oak woodlands composed of several species of oak, bay, madrone, and buckeye. Wildflowers cover the grassy hillsides in early spring.

(Continues on page 125)

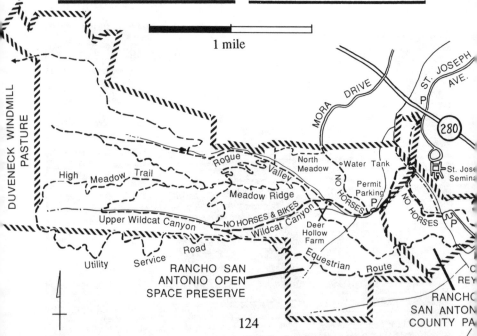

1 mile

DUVENECK WINDMILL PASTURE

MORA DRIVE

ST. JOSEPH AVE.

280

St. Jose Semina

High Meadow Trail

Rogue Valley

North Meadow

Water Tank

Permit Parking

NO HORSES

Meadow Ridge

Upper Wildcat Canyon

NO HORSES & BIKES

Wildcat Canyon

Deer Hollow Farm

NO HORSES

Utility

Service

Road

Equestrian Route

RANCHO SAN ANTONIO OPEN SPACE PRESERVE

C REY

RANCHO SAN ANTON COUNTY PA

(Continued from page 123)

Sycamores, willows, alders, box elders, and dogwoods are among the streamside trees whose foliage merges together, often covering creeks and making them invisible even from above. Trail users should take note that thorny blackberry vines, fallen tree limbs, and dense tree and shrub growth often make riperian woodlands tough to explore without trails.

The Meadow Ridge and Wildcat Canyon trails can be combined to form a pleasant loop. The rounded grassy slopes of Meadow Ridge provide sweeping views of the Santa Clara Valley and Peninsula cities to the east and north and 2800-foot Black Mountain to the west.

Being the most popular of the open space preserves, it is sometimes hard to flnd solitude. But it can be found, along with a feeling of rugged remoteness, in the western part of the preserve. For an exceptional one-way, 6-mile outing, arrange with a friend to leave a car at the Rhus Ridge Road entrance to the Duveneck Windmill Pasture Area and begin your outing at Rancho San Antonio County Park. Take the trail to Deer Hollow Farm and the Rogue Valley Trail. Turn right at the pond and climb the dirt road trail uphill,passing an ald quarry and some great views of the preserve and the Santa Clara Valley and on to the Duveneck Windmill Pasture parking lot.

For more information, call the Midpeninsula Regional Open Space District at (415) 691-1200.

The Ridge Trail

The Bay Area Ridge Trail (BART) is an ambitious 400-mile-long 9-county loop around the Bay Area. Though most of the route tends toward the wild and mountainous areas, it will also span 3 bridges across the bay and pass through the city of San Francisco and cross the Santa Clara Valley.

Much of the route is already in place through existing public parkland. The real challenge has been to flnd ways to connect these lands together with a continuous trail.

The Santa Cruz Mountains portion of the Ridge Trail climbs from the coast to Sweeney Ridge and then follows the Skyline Ridge southward. When finished it will link nearly all the trails in the range together into one vast trail network.

The entire route will be open to walkers, with alternate routes wherever feasable, for offroad bicycles and horses. The trail passes through many existing parks and preserves which are discussed in more detail in other parts of this book. For more detailed maps refer to the appropriate chapters.

For more information call the Trail Center at (415) 968-7065 or the Bay Area Ridge Trail Council at (415) 543-4291.

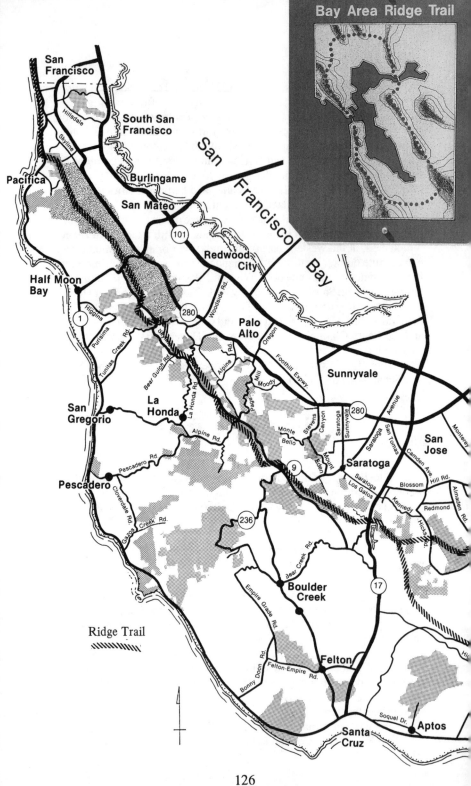

Bay Area Ridge Trail

San Francisco

South San Francisco

Hillsdale

Skyline

Burlingame

San Mateo

101

Pacifica

Redwood City

Half Moon Bay

Higgins

1

Purisima

Tunitas Creek Rd.

280

Woodside Rd.

Palo Alto

Oregon

Foothill Expwy.

Sunnyvale

San Gregorio

La Honda

Bear Gulch Rd.

La Honda Rd.

Alpine Rd.

Alpine Rd.

Moody

Monte Bello

Stevens Canyon

Saratoga

Sunnyvale

280

Avenue

Monterey

San Jose

Pescadero Rd.

9

Mount Eden

Saratoga

Los Gatos

Saratoga

San Tomas

Camden Ave.

Blossom Hill Rd.

Almaden Rd.

Pescadero

Cloverdale Rd.

Gazos Creek Rd.

236

Kennedy

Redmond

Bear Creek Rd.

Boulder Creek

17

Hicks Rd.

Ridge Trail

Empire Grade Rd.

Bonny Doon Rd.

Felton-Empire Rd.

Felton

Soquel Dr.

Aptos

Santa Cruz

San Francisco Bay

126

Russian Ridge Open Space Preserve

TO GET THERE . . . from Highway 280 take Page Mill Road uphill and west to where it intersects Skyline Boulevard. The main parking lot is at the northwest corner of the intersection. Another access is at the vista point turnoff on Skyline a little over a mile to the north.

This 1,455-acre preserve sprawls across grassy ridges and wooded valleys which can be explored by walkers, equestrians, and bicyclists by 6 miles of clearly defined trails.

Take the trail uphill from the parking lot and along the spine of the ridge. This route offers an overview of the whole preserve, visiting the highest points and unfolding a 360-degree panoramic display of Mount Tamalpais and San Francisco to the north; the bay and Mount Diablo to the east; Mount Umunhum and Monterey Bay to the south; and the ocean and Butano Ridge to the west.

This is an outstanding place to see wildflowers in the Spring. After a winter rain I found enormous spherical mushrooms more than a foot in diameter on a boulder-crowned promontory, looking very much like boulders themselves. This is also an ideal place for skiing on those rare winter days when snow mantles the hills. With its smooth, rounded forms, Russian Ridge offers miles of cross-country skiing — and some surprisingly good downhill runs too. Keep your skis ready at a moment's notice between December and February. Conditions may only be good for a few hours, usually in the early morning.

A ranch road trail descends from the ridge to Mindego Creek as it passes through grasslands and oak woodlands. Mindego Hill, the large promontory just west of the preserve, is the remnant of an ancient submarine volcano formed under the ocean more than 135 million years ago.

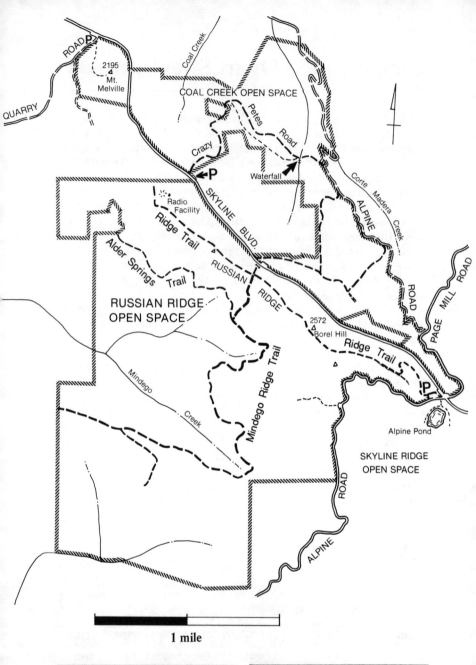

1 mile

For more information, call the Midpeninsula Regional Open Space District at (415)691-1200.

This park has exceptionally large and beautiful manzanita.

St. Joseph's Hill Open Space Preserve

TO GET THERE. . . from Highway 17 take Alma Bridge Road at Lexington Reservoir, cross the dam and park at the first parking lot on the right. To enter the park walk uphill on the dirt road across from the parking lot.

There aren't enough miles of trails in this park to keep you going for long, unless you slow down and make frequent stops to enjoy the scenery. The ranch road trail to the 1,253-foot summit of Saint Joseph's Hill is just

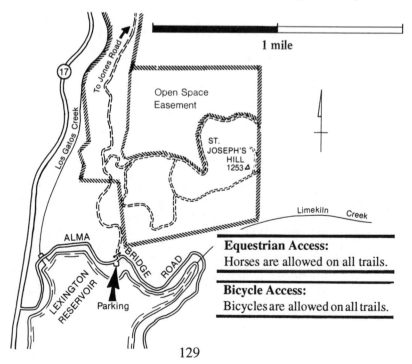

1 mile

Open Space
Easement

ST.
JOSEPH'S
HILL
1253 ▲

Limekiln Creek

Equestrian Access:
Horses are allowed on all trails.

Bicycle Access:
Bicycles are allowed on all trails.

steep enough to get the blood pulsing, but not far enough for a serious workout.

On the way up you will find increasingly attractive views of Lexington Reservoir and the surrounding mountains. The trail passes through splendid groves of exceptionally large manzanita bushes. They seem to prefer to grow in the areas of serpentine, a rock easily identified by its smooth and waxy feel.

Part of the trail is bordered by a chain link fence which keeps visitors from wandering onto property owned by The California Province of the Society of Jesus. The entire park is only 170 acres, though it seems much bigger because of the grandiose views. An additional 97 acres are retained by the Jesuits to be left undeveloped under an open space easement.

Near the summit the chaparral suddenly yields to a grassland area that the Jesuits once used as a vineyard. The top of Saint Joseph's Hill is a wonderful place for a picnic and a nap. A 360-degree panorama offers views of Mount Hamilton, the Diablo Range, and the Santa Clara Valley to the east; San Francisco Bay and the cities of the Peninsula to the north; and the ridges and peaks of the Santa Cruz Mountains and Lexington Reservoir to the west and south.

For more information contact the Midpeninsula Regional Open Space District at (415) 691-1200.

Sam McDonald County Park

TO GET THERE. . .take La Honda-Pescadero Road about 3 miles west of La Honda.

This is a beautiful 995 acres of redwoods and an ideal destination for a picnic and a hike. The park is kept in a semi-primitive state by limiting automobile access only to the park office area off Pescadero Road. Three walk-in campgrounds, available by reservation, range in distance from .5 to about 1 mile from the parking lot.

The Forest Loop Trail is a good 3.1-mile hike northwest from the parking lot, and though not very long, this peaceful redwood garden of sorrel and ferns has plenty of scenic diversions and its share of challenging ups and downs. The continuation of the Forest Loop Trail beginning on the other side of the parking lot is equally rewarding. This part of the trail continues as a dirt road for about 2 miles southwest from Pescadero Road and passes some splendid first-growth redwoods, the most magnificent of which can be seen along the short footpath that crosses and then returns back to the dirt road.

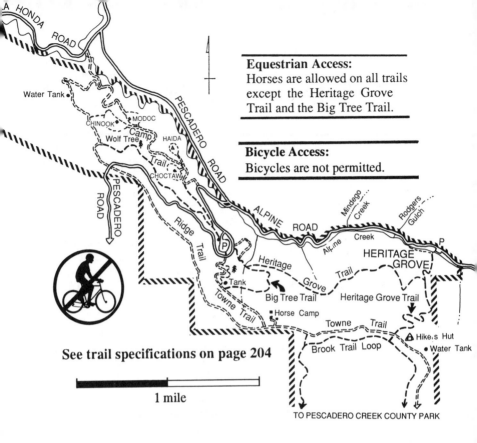

A HONDA ROAD

Water Tank

CHINOOK MODOC
Wolf Tree Camp.
  HAIDA

Trail
CHOCTAW

PESCADERO ROAD

PESCADERO ROAD

Ridge Trail

P

Towne Trail

Tank

Heritage

Grove

Trail

Big Tree Trail

Horse Camp

ALPINE ROAD

Mindego Creek

Alpine Creek

Rodgers Gulch

P

HERITAGE GROVE

Heritage Grove Trail

Towne Trail

Brook Trail Loop

Hike.s Hut

Water Tank

TO PESCADERO CREEK COUNTY PARK

Equestrian Access:
Horses are allowed on all trails except the Heritage Grove Trail and the Big Tree Trail.

Bicycle Access:
Bicycles are not permitted.

See trail specifications on page 204

1 mile

The Sierra Club's hikers hut is a great place to stay.

You can travel by trail from Sam McDonald to Pescadero Creek County Park, San Mateo County Memorial Park, and Portola State Park. The route is about 6 miles from Sam McDonald park headquarters to San Mateo County Memorial Park, and a little more than 7 miles to Portola State Park. This route climbs past first and second-growth redwoods to grassy hilltop vistas and then descends into a forest of Douglas fir and second-growth redwoods. When you get to the top of the ridge, in the grassy meadow, head south on Brook Trail or Towne Fire Road to Pomponio Trail. Head west to San Mateo County Memorial Park and east to Portola State Park, or combine Brook Trail, Pomponio Trail, and Towne Fire Road together into a scenic 8-mile loop ramble.

For an exceptional 4.1 mile loop, begin at the ranger station and take the Big Tree Trail across the road and uphill to the Heritage Grove Trail, which continues 2.6 miles to the small but beautiful Heritage Grove of old-growth redwoods. From there head uphill to the Towne Fire Road and an optional stopoff at the Sierra Club's hikers hut. Then take the Towne Fire Road west and downhill back to where you began.

Sam McDonald (1884-1957) was a popular Stanford University employee who owned the property until his death. He loved nature and willed that his forest be preserved in its natural state. Stanford owned the land until it became a county park in 1969.

Individuals or groups with horses can reserve the Jack Brook Horse Camp for overnight outings between April 15 and November 15. Corrals, picnic tables, and barbeques are available.

Organized youth groups can reserve sites at Modoc, Chinook, and Choctow Youth Group Areas.

For more information and reservations for group camping, call park headquarters at (415)879-0212 or (415)363-4021.

Heritage Grove:

This 37-acre, old-growth redwood grove is part of Sam McDonald Park and can be reached by taking the Heritage Grove Trail from park headquarters or from the hikers' hut or by driving east to a parking lot on Alpine Road one mile from its intersection with Pescadero Road. This magnificent grove was scheduled to be logged until a citizens group raised funds and purchased the land. The loggers' paint marks can still be seen on some of the trees they intended to remove.

San Bruno Mountain County Park

TO GET THERE... From Bayshore Boulevard in Brisbane, turn west on Guadalupe Canyon Parkway.

This 1,314 foot high promontory is a grassland island in an urban sea and is the only large open space in this densely settled and industrialized area. It's an ecological remnant of northern San Mateo County and a wonderful wildflower garden in spring. Actually, this "mountain" consists of 2 parallel ridges separated by the Guadalupe Valley.

April wildflowers here are exceptional both in abundance and diversity. Perhaps the best wildflower walk is the 3.1 mile Summit Loop Trail, which begins at the parking lot just south of Guadalupe Canyon Parkway and climbs 725 feet to the summit. This route is notable for striking vistas down the mountain and north to San Francisco. Along the

Equestrian Access:
Horses are allowed on all trails except the disabled trail and the Bog Trail. Unload horses at day camp or the other parking lot just to the south.

Bicycle Access:
Bicycles are only allowed on the Old Guadalupe Trail, the Saddle Loop Trail, Radio Road, and the Day Camp Access Trail.

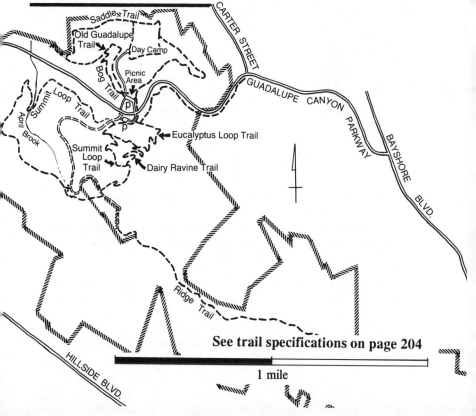

See trail specifications on page 204

1 mile

way the trail dips into a steep canyon along April Brook, a place known as "The Flower Garden" for its extraordinary springtime flowers.

Most of the mountain is covered with coastal scrub vegetation and with annual grasses that make it green in the winter and spring and golden brown in summer. Most of the trees are in the canyons and on north-facing slopes. A few coastal wood, bracken, and chain ferns dwell in moist and shady places.

Surrounded by dense urban development, this 4-mile-long mountain is an ecological island that supports a unique community of plants and animals. The mission blue butterfly, the San Bruno elfin butterfly, and several species of manzanita are unique to this area. Fourteen species of plants growing here are classifled as rare and endangered .

Walk for Health

Our bodies are perfectly designed for walking. There is no other form of exercise that is safer or more beneficial.

Vigorous walking maintains the heart muscle in healthy tone, lowers blood pressure, controls weight, reduces tension, headaches, and backaches; and it even benefits the heart and lungs every bit as much as jogging.

A Veterans Administration study of elderly people found that a walking program actually resulted in improved memory, vision, and reasoning power.

Doctors recommend taking a post-walk stroll for a few minutes after a vigorous outing to give the heart a chance to slow down gradually.

San Francisco Fish & Game Refuge

If you've ever gazed into the land around Crystal Springs and San Andreas lakes while driving on Highway 280 and wished it were possible to get in there to explore, then you may be interested to know that there is some limited access. Because the city of San Francisco jealously guards the purity of its drinking water the walkways through this 23,000-acre watershed are wide and bordered with barbed wire fences, and some are paved.

The reservoir was named for the Crystal Springs Hotel which occupied the valley before the dam was built in 1896.

Schools and educational groups, however, may obtain permits to visit other areas of the property for nature study. Applications for permits should be filed at least 2 weeks in advance by contacting the San Francisco Water Department at 1000 El Camino Real, Millbrae, CA 94030; (415) 872-5900 .

The majestic Pulgas Water Temple, on the Crystal Springs Trail, is where Yosemite water enters Crystal Springs Reservoir.

Crystal Springs Trail:

The Crystal Springs Trail connects Huddart Park with Highway 92. Unfortunately, there is still a 1.6-mile gap between Highway 92 and the Sawyer Camp Trail. It goes from Huddart to Raymundo Road and resumes a fifth of a mile up the road, paralleling Highway 280 and Canada Road. From the parking lot at the north end of the trail, at Highway 92 just east of where it crosses the reservoir, the trail heads south 4 miles to the parking lot at the intersection of Edgewood Road and Canada Road. This route passes the historic Pulgas Water Temple. From the Edgewood/Canada parking lot you can go south by trail 2.4 miles south to Huddart Park.

This route is popular with equestrians, though many walkers won't like the flatness and tameness of the route, or the sights and sounds of traffic on Highway 280 and Canada Road.

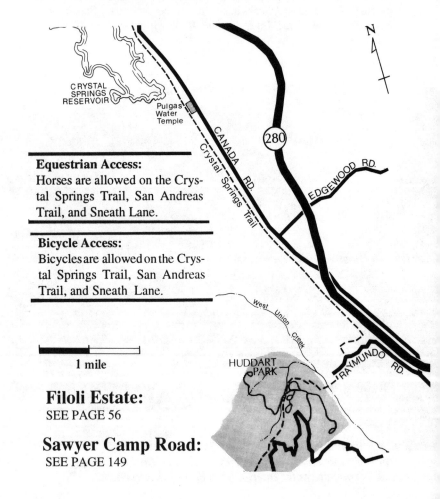

Equestrian Access:
Horses are allowed on the Crystal Springs Trail, San Andreas Trail, and Sneath Lane.

Bicycle Access:
Bicycles are allowed on the Crystal Springs Trail, San Andreas Trail, and Sneath Lane.

1 mile

Filoli Estate:
SEE PAGE 56

Sawyer Camp Road:
SEE PAGE 149

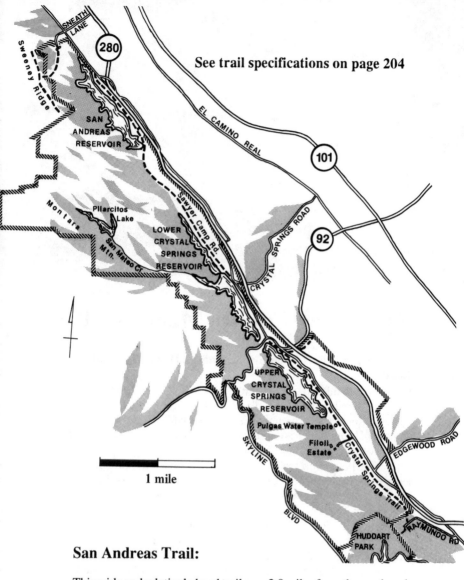

See trail specifications on page 204

San Andreas Trail:

This wide and relatively level trail runs 2.9 miles from the north end of the Sawyer Camp Road, at Hillcrest, to Skyline Boulevard. Most of the trail is paved.

Sneath Lane;

From Highway 280 in San Bruno, take Sneath Lane west all the way to the locked gate. The paved road continues through the San Francisco watershed property, with barbed wire on both sides, and up the Sweeney Ridge unit of the Golden Gate National Recreation Area. This route offers great views of San Andreas Reservoir.

San Mateo County Memorial Park

TO GET THERE... It's southwest of Sam McDonald Park on Pescadero Road.

Visitors to this park may swim in Pescadero Creek, camp, picnic amid old-growth redwoods, and walk about 10 miles of trails.

The Mount Ellen Summit Trail-Lower Nature Trail Loop around the summit of Mount Ellen is a scenic route involving a climb of about 400 feet and a distance of less than 2 miles.

The Pomponio Trail takes you on a 3.5-mile loop north of Pescadero Road as it climbs above the redwoods and into the Douglas fir, chaparral, and oak. This route offers great views of the Pescadero Creek Valley and the ocean.

If you're looking for something a bit more challenging than Memorial Park has to offer, try walking to Portola State Park or Sam McDonald County Park, both about 6 miles away. For information on routes to these parks see the chapters on Pescadero Creek and Sam McDonald County Parks.

Sawmill owner Edwin Peterson bought a tract of old-growth redwoods at the present site of San Mateo County Memorial Park. He would have logged the area it it hadn't been for Roy W. Cloud, county superintendent of schools. When Cloud visited the nearby Wurr School in 1923 he was so impressed by the magnificent forest he presented a plan to save it to the county board of supervisors. The 310 acres were purchased for $70,000.

This park has some of the best picnicking and camping facilities in the Santa Cruz Mountains. There are 140 family campsites, available on a first-come, first-served basis. for more information, call (415)879-0212.

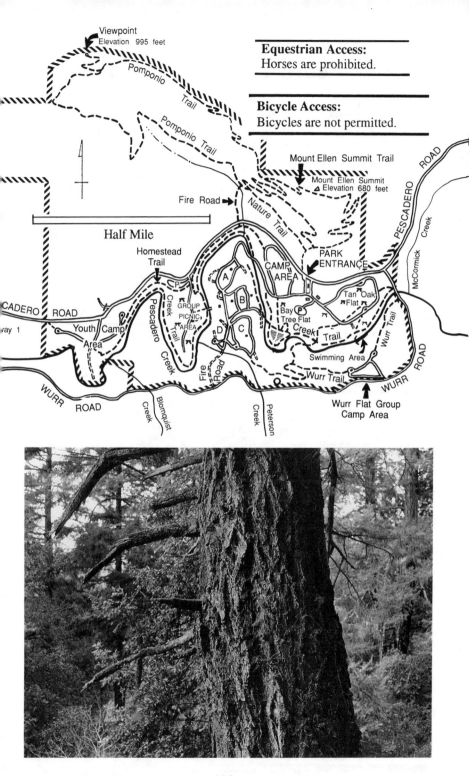

San Pedro Valley County Park

TO GET THERE. . .take Highway 1 to Pacifica, heading southeast on Linda Mar Boulevard to Oddstad Boulevard. Public parking and park access are next to Saint Peters Catholic Church.

This park is a 1,000 acres of coastal scrub and chaparral, with a few grassy places and riperian woodlands for diversity. You can get an easy look at it by taking the nearly level Weiler Ranch Trail along the Middle Fork of San Pedro Creek.

Keep an eye open for the Valley View Trail that switchbacks up the hillside from Weiler Ranch Trail, climbing about 600 feet to some nice views of the San Pedro Valley and winding around the hills for 1.6 miles and back to the dirt road.

The middle and south forks of San Pedro Creek flow year around and are among the few remaining spawning areas of steelhead trout in San Mateo County, especially from December to February. Views of

Equestrian Access:
Horses are allowed on all trails except the Brooks Creek Trail and Brooks Falls View Trail.

Bicycle Access:
Bicycles are only allowed on the Weiler Ranch Road Trail.

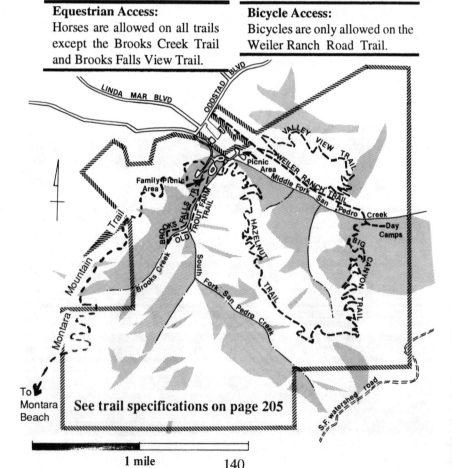

See trail specifications on page 205

1 mile

140

Brooks Falls, which drops 175 feet in 3 tiers, may be enjoyed during the rainy season.

The Montara Mountain Trail climbs 1,400 feet in 2.5 miles as it enters McNee Ranch State Park (see page 95). It then intersects the service Road, where you can take a 1-mile detour to enjoy great views from the top of Montara Mountain.

The Hazelnut Trail, Big Canyon Trail, and Weiler Ranch Trail can be combined to form a spectacularly scenic loop of about 4.3 miles and an elevation gain of about 800 feet..

Other common coastal scrub vegetation includes: monkeyflower, shrubby lupine, ceanothus, coastal sage scrub, and thimbleberry. This vegetation thrives in the coastal zone where steady ocean winds sweep the land and make life difficult for most trees. Along the park's small creeks you will notice dense stands of willows, which shelter a ground cover which includes poison hemlock, blackberry vines, horsetails, and bracken ferns.

This park has a group picnic area and family picnic sites with barbecue pits. Reservations are required for all youth groups, regardless of size or activity. The group picnic area is open by reservation, which may be obtained by calling (415) 363-4021. For other park information, call (415) 355-8289.

Sanborn Skyline County Park

TO GET THERE... take Highway 9 (Big Basin Way) west of Saratoga and turn south on Sanborn Road. The Lake Ranch area may be reached by taking Black Road 1.5 miles east from Skyline Boulevard.
    Sanborn Skyline County Park covers 2,856 acres on the steep east side of the range and has scenic trails, excellent picnicking facilities, a walk-in campground, and one of the Bay Area's best hostels. From the park's many scenic overlooks you can gaze down on the smoggy haze that often covers San Jose and instead be glad to be in the mountains.

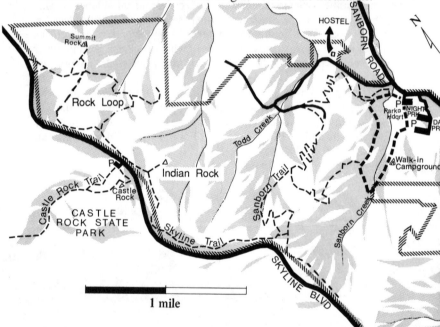

    The park has 2 entrances from Sanborn Road, one for day use and another for camping. There are 42 campsites on the Sanborn Trail, available on a first-come, first-served basis. To camp at these sites park at the overnight parking lot, register at the nearby park headquarters, and walk the short distance uphill from the parking lot to the camping area. Each family campsite has a picnic table, a fire place, and restrooms nearby.
    Be sure to visit the natural history exhibit at the visitor center and Youth Science Institute.
    Park headquarters are in an interesting sandstone and redwood house built in 1912. Nearby is a self-guided nature trail. The dirt road, which begins at the parking lot, continues uphill past the campground and

The old Welch-Hurst House (1908) has been thoughtfully renovated and is now one of the Bay Area's most attractive and comfortable hostels. It's a wonderful getaway from the city, and a place to meet travelers from around the world. It was built as a hunting lodge by Judge James Welch.

See trail specifications on page 204

Equestrian Access:
Horses are allowed on the Skyline Trail, the Rock Loop, and the Sanborn Trail.

Bicycle Access:
Bicycles are not permitted.

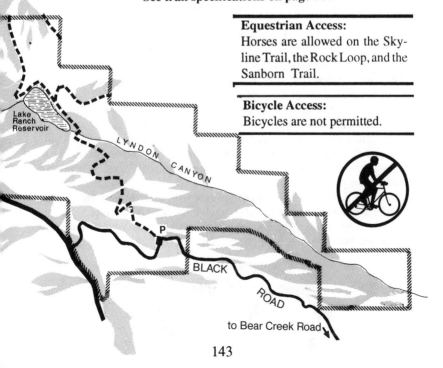

climbs nearly 1,700 feet in about 3 miles to Skyline Boulevard near the summit of the ridge. This route offers beautiful views of the Santa Clara Valley and passes through several different ecological zones. Second-growth redwoods predominate in the shady canyon bottom around park headquarters. Douglas fir, tanoak, bay, and madrone becomes increasingly common in the higher and drier areas where the trail approaches Skyline Boulevard.

The Sanborn Trail may be used as an extension to the "Skyline-to-the-Sea" Trail by parking at the overnight parking lot and hiking west on the Sanborn Trail and north on the Skyline Trail, which connects with Castle Rock State Park. The Castle Rock Trail Camp is an additional 3.2 miles on the Castle Rock Trail, which connects with the "Skyline-to-the-Sea" Trail via the Travertine Springs Trail.

The Skyline Trail goes to Indian Rock and connects with the Summit Rock Trail which goes to Summit Rock, a sandstone counterpart to Castle Rock and a good place to climb around and explore. It offers a spectacular view of the Santa Clara Valley and has some interesting shallow caves.

This park has one of the most unusual and interesting Youth Hostels in the state. Built of redwood logs, the historic Welch-Hurst House (1908) is about as rustic as anyplace can be, and makes an ideal getaway from the city. Thoughtfully renovated, the inside is comfortable and has many modern conveniences. The log house is in a shadowy grove of redwoods, which also has picnic tables, a barbeque, a wonderful old gazebo, and a duck pond. The hostel is open all year from 5 pm. to 9 a.m. For more information call (408) 741-9555, or (408) 298-0670.

Lake Ranch Unit

The Lake Ranch Reservoir is an easy 1.3 miles from Black Road. You can stop here and have lunch with the newts, who consider this a favorite hangout. As of this writing the land connecting the reservoir area with the southern end of Sanborn Road is expected to be added to the park soon. Call park headquarters for current information.

The terrain here is steep and the mountains are wooded with bay, Douglas fir, oak, maple, madrone, and redwood. Just east of the dirt road is the canyon abyss of the San Andreas Fault rift zone, where two continental plates collide.

The San Andreas Fault cuts a linear rift valley through this park. It runs along Lyndon Canyon and through Lake Ranch Reservoir.

Except for registered camping, the park is open from 8 a.m. until sundown. For more information, call (408) 867-9959.

Model plane flying is one of the activities available at Santa Teresa.

Santa Teresa County Park

TO GET THERE . . . take Bernal Road southwest from Highway 101.

Above the south-bounding amorphous sprawl of San Jose, this gentle, grassy park is witness to the dramatic urbanization that is transforming this part of the Santa Clara Valley. Housing tracts and industry sprout at its feet at this narrow part of the valley, making Santa Teresa an important urban recreation area.

Equestrian Access:
Horses are allowed on all trails except the Ohlone Hiking Trail.

Bicycle Access:
Bicycles are only allowed on the Bicycle Trail.

See trail specifications on page 205

1 mile

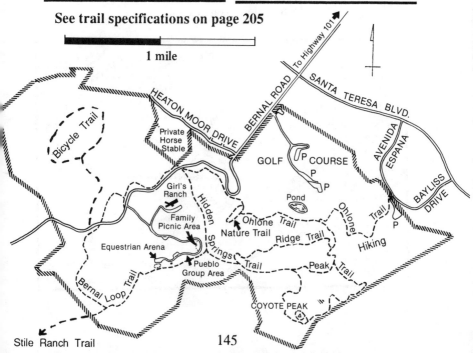

Santa Teresa County Park is 1,006 acres of low grassy hills capped by rocky outcroppings which offer views of the Santa Clara Valley immediately below, and Mount Hamilton and the Diablo Range in the distance. The trails here are easy and relaxed; perfect for a picnic. Scattered stands of oak and bay punctuate the grassy hills, which turn brilliant green between January and May, yet are roasted brown by late May as if — as John Muir noted — every leaf and blade had been baked in an oven.

Santa Teresa has excellent equestrian trails, lots of group picnic facilities, a fishing pond, a field archery range, an eighteen-hole golf course, and a field for operating radio-controlled miniature airplanes.

This park has group and family picnic areas, a children's fishing pond, and an equestrian assembly area.

For more information call (408)225-0225.

Stile Ranch Trail:

This segment of the Bay Area Ridge Trail can be started from the McKean Road or Fortini Road trailheads. It runs through the San Jose city parks along Alamitos and Calero creeks and climbs east and north into Santa Teresa County Park.

Part of the trail goes through IBM's Almaden Research Facility serpentine grassland and chaparral slopes which are great for viewing wildflowers in April. Along the way are views of Mount Umunhum and Loma Prieta. Look for an historic stone wall built by Chinese workers in the nineteenth century.

Horses and bicycles are allowed on this trail.

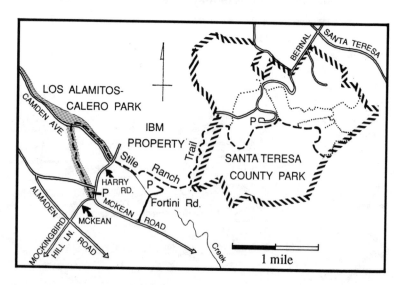

Saratoga Gap Open Space Preserve

TO GET THERE... The trail through this preserve can be started at Saratoga Gap near the northeast corner of the intersection of Skyline Boulevard and Highway 9. This trail continues north through Upper Stevens Creek County Park and Monte Bello Open Space Preserve.

Saratoga Gap Open Space Preserve is at the northeast corner of Saratoga Gap. The trail through this 492 acre park parallels Skyline Boulevard, crossing grassy hills that explode with wildflowers in early spring. The route then enters 1095-acre Upper Stevens Creek County Park and dips into the steep, shady canyon that contains the cool and perennial waters of Stevens Creek. You will find many impressive vistas along this trail and see beautiful stands of bay trees, madrone, and canyon live, coast live, and black oak. The Stevens Creek canyon is forested largely with Douglas fir and with big-leaf maple along the creek. The banks of this bouncing, bubbling creek make an excellent picnic stop.

The trail climbs the other slope of the canyon, following a dirt road and rising to the oak and bay studded grasslands of Monte Bello Ridge. Monte Bello Open Space Preserve contains 3258 acres and can be reached from Saratoga Gap via the trail previously described or from Page Mill Road.

There are 3 parks that can be combined to form a grand and diverse hiking adventure of nearly 8 miles from Saratoga Gap to Page Mill Road and Los Trancos Open Space Preserve. Unless you want to hike another 8 miles back, use 2 cars and at least 1 friend and leave a car at Page Mill Road to shuttle back to the trailhead. This hike passes through Saratoga Gap Open Space Preserve, Upper Stevens Creek County Park, and Monte Bello Open Space Preserve. Just north of Page Mill Road is Los Trancos Open Space Preserve. This route explores grassy ridges, chaparral, oak woodlands, and forests of Douglas fir, and involves an elevation range of about 1,400 feet.

For more information, call the Midpeninsula Regional Open Space District at (415) 949-5500.

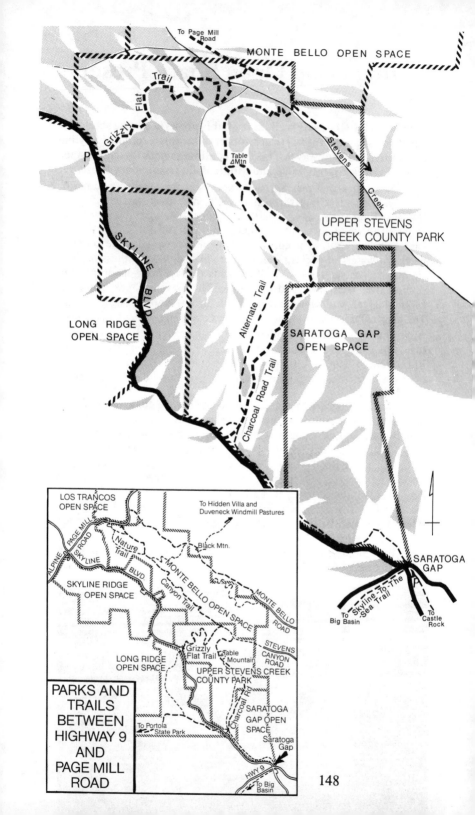

MONTE BELLO OPEN SPACE

To Page Mill Road

Grizzly Flat Trail

Table Mtn

Stevens Creek

UPPER STEVENS CREEK COUNTY PARK

SKYLINE BLVD

P

LONG RIDGE OPEN SPACE

Alternate Trail

Charcoal Road Trail

SARATOGA GAP OPEN SPACE

SARATOGA GAP

P

To Skyline-To-The-Sea Trail

To Big Basin

To Castle Rock

LOS TRANCOS OPEN SPACE

To Hidden Villa and Duveneck Windmill Pastures

PAGE MILL ROAD

ALPINE

SKYLINE BLVD

Nature Trail

Black Mtn.

MONTE BELLO OPEN SPACE

SKYLINE RIDGE OPEN SPACE

Canyon Trail

MONTE BELLO ROAD

LONG RIDGE OPEN SPACE

Grizzly Flat Trail

Table Mountain

UPPER STEVENS CREEK COUNTY PARK

STEVENS CANYON ROAD

Charcoal Rd.

SARATOGA GAP OPEN SPACE

Saratoga Gap

To Portola State Park

HWY 9

To Big Basin

PARKS AND TRAILS BETWEEN HIGHWAY 9 AND PAGE MILL ROAD

148

Sawyer Camp Trail

TO GET THERE... The southern access is at the intersection of Skyline Boulevard and Crystal Springs Road. Southbound from Highway 280 take Black Mountain Road offramp. Northbound, take Bunker Hill Drive exit. The northern end is at Hillcrest Boulevard, which can be reached southbound on Highway 280 via the larkspur Drive exit on northbound via the Millbrae Avenue exit.

This is the most popular trail in the Santa Cruz Mountains. With more than 200,000 visitors a year this 6-mile route can be pretty crowded on weekends with walkers, joggers, bicyclists, and equestrians.

This scenic trail, which is actually a paved road now closed to motor vehicles, passes along the east side of Lower Crystal Springs Reservoir and San Andreas Lake. The easy access to peninsula cities, combined with striking backdrops of water and mountains makes it easy to overlook the fact that the entire route is bordered by barbed wire to keep trail users from wandering onto San Francisco watershed land.

North of Crystal Springs Reservoir the trail straddles the San Andreas Fault and passes an enormous bay tree, called the Jepson Bay, one of the oldest and largest in the area.

The trail is named for a camp where Leander Sawyer trained performing horses for circuses in the 1870's.

The trail is open from sunrise until sunset. Facilities include picnic tables, restrooms, and telephones.

To reduce conflict among trail users a 5 m.p.h. speed limit is set for bicycles on the first half mile of the trail at each end. The rest of the trail has a 15 m.p.h. speed limit.

For more information, call San Mateo County Parks Department at (415) 363-4021.

The Jepson Bay Laurel, along the Sawyer Camp Trail, is one of the largest of its species in the state. There are picnic tables nearby.

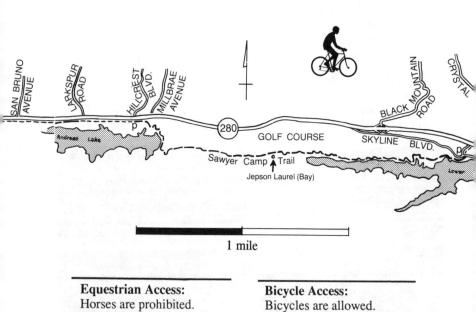

Equestrian Access:
Horses are prohibited.

Bicycle Access:
Bicycles are allowed.

Sierra Azul Open Space Preserve

In the rugged and dry part of the Santa Cruz Mountains east of Highway 17, the Sierra Azul (Spanish for "Blue Range") has access in 2 units of the 9,550-acre Sierra Azul Open Space Preserve. For more information call the Midpeninsula Regional Open Space District at (415) 691-1200.

Kennedy Road Access

TO GET THERE . . . take Highway 17 to Los Gatos, head southeast on Saratoga-Los Gatos Road and turn left on Los Gatos Boulevard. Turn right on Kennedy Road and continue about 2.4 miles to the park entrance at its intersection with Top Of The Hill Road. The entrance trail begins just to the left of a private driveway which is across from the intersection.

A well-maintained dirt road serves as a good trail for a climb of about 1600 feet to the top of the ridge.

Along the way you will pass steep and wooded canyons filled with oak, bay, and maple, and views of ever-increasing splendor reveal Mount Hamilton and the Diablo Range, San Jose, and the Santa Clara Valley. The scenery gets increasingly wild and remote as you climb higher on this chaparral-clad ridge.

At the beginning of the trail is an abandoned apricot orchard that still bears a bountiful harvest of delicious fruit around late June and early July. Be prepared for warm weather in summer and little water. Poison oak is common, but easily avoided. This unit covers 467 acres.

Lexington Reservoir Access

TO GET THERE . . . take Highway 17 south of Los Gatos to the

Lexington Reservoir. Take Alma Bridge Road about 1.6 miles to where the trail begins at a green metal gate.

The 900-foot ascent to Priest Rock begins with the oak woods, but soon enters the nearly shadeless realm of chaparral. During the warm summer months this trail will seem particularly formidable, and unless you bring plenty of water the only moisture you will find anywhere will be perspiration. If you make it to the top and back on a warm day reward yourself with a dip in the reservoir.

The upper parts of this 844-acre unit have few trees, but lots of views. Look for Mount Hamilton, the Santa Clara Valley, San Francisco Bay, and the Skyline Ridge.

In a chaparral area such as this, where dense brush makes travel difficult, wildlife as well as people use the trails and dirt roads. Look for signs of coyotes, deer, bobcats, and others. While walking up this trail I came around a bend and was suddenly confronted with a wild pig and her 5 young.

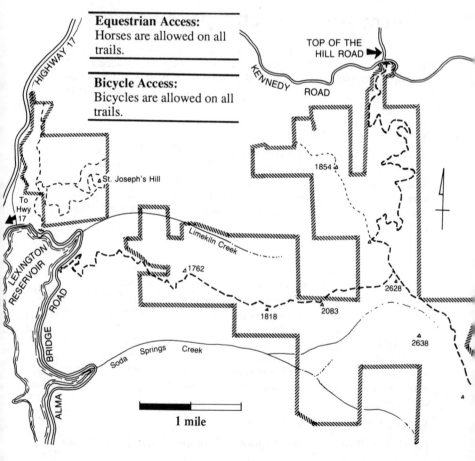

MOUNT UMUNHUM AREA

TO GET THERE... from Highway 17 take Camden Road south, turn right on Hicks Road and continue 6.3 miles to where it intersects Mount Umunhum Road. Take this private road uphill, to the west, 1.8 miles and park near the locked gate. Another part of the preserve may be reached by driving 1.2 miles up Reynolds Road to a gate.

This rugged land of steep ravines and breathtaking views forms a 6,000-acre patchwork of open space astride the Sierra Azul Range.

The only access through the preserve and to the 3,486-foot summit of Mount Umunhum is by way of a two lane paved road built by the U.S. Air Force on a non-exclusive easement over private land. It provided access to the radar tower of the former Almaden Air Force Station on Mount Umunhum. The top of the mountain will be closed to the public until the air force gets around to toxic waste cleanup and removal of safety hazards.

Mount Umunhum, one of the most prominent features of the Santa Cruz Mountains, means hummingbird in the Ohlone Indian language and was considered to be one of their 4 sacred Bay Area peaks.

The Bald Mountain parcel of this preserve is easily accessible to the public without walking on asphalt. Park just off the road near the stop sign at the locked gate and follow the dirt road that heads to the southeast and up the grassy hilltop. This 2,387-foot rounded summit is an easy half-mile walk to a place that is perfect for picnicking and kite flying. It is also one

As a taxpayer you have a right to drive up Mount Umunhum Road to visit Bald Mountain.

of the few places in the vicinity not covered with chaparral. Dramatic views of the Sierra Azul Range and the Santa Clara Valley are among the best reasons to visit.

The Reynolds Road area is small, but it is ideal for easy walks and a picnic. In the shadow of Mount Umunhum, this parcel offers rolling hills and oak woods.

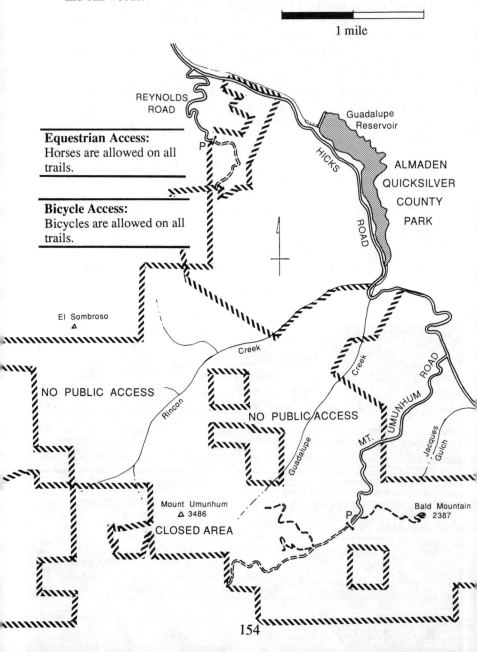

1 mile

REYNOLDS ROAD

Guadalupe Reservoir

HICKS ROAD

ALMADEN QUICKSILVER COUNTY PARK

Equestrian Access:
Horses are allowed on all trails.

Bicycle Access:
Bicycles are allowed on all trails.

El Sombroso △

NO PUBLIC ACCESS

Creek

Rincon

Creek

Guadalupe Creek

MT. UMUNHUM ROAD

Jacques Gulch

NO PUBLIC ACCESS

Mount Umunhum △ 3486

CLOSED AREA

P

Bald Mountain 2387

154

Skyline Ridge Open Space Preserve

TO GET THERE... From Highway 280 take Page Mill Road uphill and west to where it intersects Skyline Boulevard and turns into Alpine Road. To explore the Alpine Pond area park at the Russian Ridge Open Space parking lot on Alpine Road just west of Skyline Boulevard. The main entrance is about a mile south on Skyline Boulevard.

Tranquil ponds, deep forested canyons, rounded mountain peaks with great views, and an extensive network of trails make this an ideal destination for hikers, equestrians, and off-road bicyclists.

The half-mile footpath around Alpine Pond is the easiest trail in the preserve. Horseshoe Lake, to the south, is also easy to reach and is a pleasant setting for a picnic. This 27-foot-deep springfed reservoir, named for its shape, is inhabited by bluegill and bass and is a rest stop for migrating waterfowl. Fishing and boating are not allowed.

For a more vigorous outing, head uphill from either pond, passing ancient oaks and steep grasslands that yield broad vistas of the Pescadero Creek watershed and Butano Ridge to the west, Monte Bello Ridge to the east, and Loma Prieta-- the highest peak in the Santa Cruz Mountains-- to the south. The highest point at Skyline Ridge is 2,493 feet.

The original Page Mill Road west of Skyline Boulevard was built by William Page in 1868 to transport lumber from his mill in what is now Portola State Park to Palo Alto. The Skyline Ranch was a retreat for Governor James Rolph in the 1930's.

Because of its magnificent setting and easy connection with other preserves the open space district is making Skyline Ridge an open space showcase as the christmas trees are phased out.

This 1,254-acre preserve is an important part of the Skyline open space corridor, and is a key link in the developing Ridge Trail through San Mateo and Santa Clara Counties. This preserve is part of more than 7,500-acres of contiguous open space and parkland on this part of the Skyline Ridge area. For more information, call the Midpeninsula Regional Open Space District at (415) 691-1200.

Equestrian Access:	**Bicycle Access:**
Horses are allowed where indicated on map.	Bicycles are allowed where indicated on map.

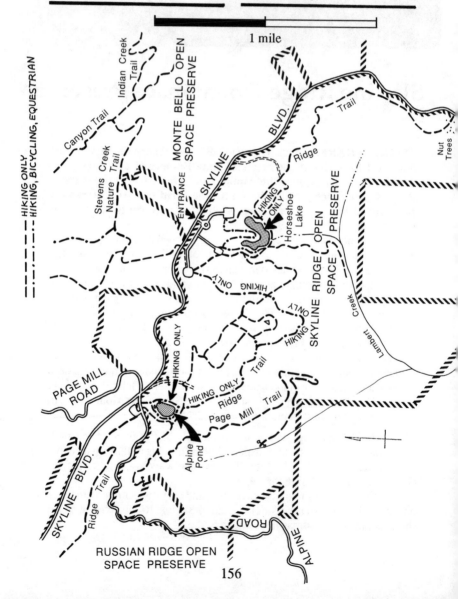

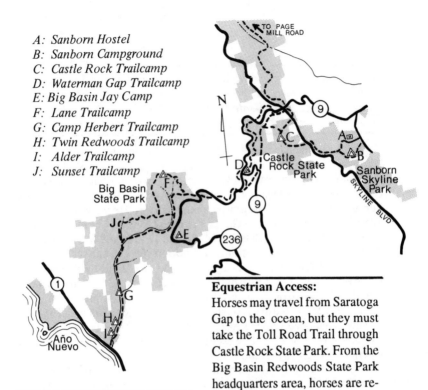

A: Sanborn Hostel
B: Sanborn Campground
C: Castle Rock Trailcamp
D: Waterman Gap Trailcamp
E: Big Basin Jay Camp
F: Lane Trailcamp
G: Camp Herbert Trailcamp
H: Twin Redwoods Trailcamp
I: Alder Trailcamp
J: Sunset Trailcamp

Bicycle Access:
Bicycles are only allowed on the southernmost part of this route, in Big Basin Redwoods State Park south of Berry Creek.

Equestrian Access:
Horses may travel from Saratoga Gap to the ocean, but they must take the Toll Road Trail through Castle Rock State Park. From the Big Basin Redwoods State Park headquarters area, horses are required to follow the Hihn Hammond Road over Mount McAbee and connect with the "Skyline-to-the-Sea" Trail south of Berry Creek.

Skyline-to-the-Sea Trail

TO GET THERE ... the trail begins at the intersection of Skyline and Highway 9, or at Highway I at Waddell Creek. It can be extended through Castle Rock State Park, Sanborn Skyline County Park, and Monte Bello Open Space Preserve.

Skyline to Big Basin:

The "Skyline-to-the-Sea" Trail offers real backpacking opportunities from Saratoga Gap or Castle Rock State Park to Big Basin Redwoods State Park and on to the coast.

The total distance from Saratoga Gap to the ocean is about 28 miles. The trail passes through grasslands, chaparral, and forests of oak, madrone, Douglas fir and redwoods, and impressive vistas are common along the route.

The trailhead at Saratoga Gap (where Skyline Boulevard intersects Highway 9) is on the south side of Highway 9 just west of Skyline. From the Castle Rock State Park trailcamp the trail crosses Skyline twice before connecting the trailhead at Saratoga Gap or by taking the Travertine Springs Trail shortcut. The trail parallels Highway 9 for about 7 miles from Saratoga Gap to Waterman Gap campground. The distance to Waterman Gap from the Castle Rock trailhead is about 11 to 15 miles, depending on the route. The Travertine Springs Trail offers the most direct route.

The "Skyline-to-the-Sea" trail, which was built by thousands of volunteers in 1969, closely parallels highways 9 and 236 because this land was already owned by the state. Hikers and equestrians who prefer straying farther from the sound of traffic should try the Toll Road south of Highway 9. This abandoned logging road, built in 1871, connects with the main "Skyline-to-the-Sea" route west of Saratoga Gap and again west of the junction of Highways 9 and 236.

The trail continues for about 9.5 miles from Waterman Gap to Big Basin Park Headquarters. From China Grade Road the trail passes through chaparral and stands of knobcone pine and enters the shady redwood groves along Opal Creek. Just before the trail drops into Big Basin, you will be greeted by splendid views of the mountains to the southwest.

Due to a lack of water on parts of the trail during the dry season, hikers are advised to bring water. The Castle Rock campground has water, pit toilets, and fireplaces. The Waterman Gap campground has water, pit toilets, and does not permit ground fires. The Big Basin Jay camp has water, flush toilets, fireplaces, and showers. For campsite information, call park headquarters at (408) 338-6132.

Big Basin to the Sea:

The "Skyline-to-the-Sea" Trail follows Waddell Creek through the 1,700-acre "Rancho Del Oso" part of the park and on to the coast. From the ridge west of park headquarters the trail follows Waddell Creek all the way to Highway 1. A short sidetrip up the Berry Creek Falls Trail will reward you with 2 of the great wonders of the Santa Cruz Mountains: Berry Creek and Silver falls. The distance from park headquarters to the trailhead near Highway I is about 10.5 miles on the "Skyline-to-the-Sea" trail, about 11 miles on the Howard King Trail, and about 12 miles on the Sunset Trail. The "Skyline-to-the-Sea" route has the easiest grade of the 3 trails. Travelers on the Sunset Trail may want to make camp at Sunset Trailcamp, which is about 5.5 miles from park headquarters and upstream from Berry Creek Falls.

There are 3 trailcamps in "Rancho Del Oso": Camp Herbert is about 7.5 miles from Big Basin park headquarters; Twin Redwoods is 1.5 miles downstream from Camp Herbert; and Alder Camp is less than half a mile downstream. Ground fires are prohibited and campers are encouraged to make reservations by calling Big Basin park headquarters at (408) 338-6132. There is a camping fee.

This beautiful canyon was an ideal place for the Ohlone Indians, who gathered marine edibles from the coast and stalked game in the mountains. Mammals you may see here include coyotes, racoons, deer, bobcats, foxes, weasels, possums, skunks, several species of squirrels, chipmunks, and an assortment of other rodents. This is still an important feeding and nesting area for birds, with more than 200 species sighted. Near the trail is the Eagle Tree, an impressive first-growth redwood which once hosted an eagle nest.

The "Skyline-to-the-Sea" Trail is the hub of a vast network of trails developing in this part of the Santa Cruz Mountains. It is possible to hike about 8.5 miles from Los Trancos Open Space Preserve on Page Mill Road to Saratoga Gap, where you can connect with the "Skyline-to-the-Sea" Trail. To hike from one side of the range to the other, park at Sanborn-Skyline County Park and take the Sanborn and Skyline trails to Castle Rock State Park and on to Saratoga Gap via the Castle Rock Trail.

See the Big Basin and Castle Rock chapters for more detailed maps and information .

Saratoga Gap—Waterman Gap Trailcamp: 7 miles
Waterman Gap Trailcamp Big Basin Jay Camp: 9.5 miles
Big Basin Jay Camp—Camp Herbert: 7.5 miles
Camp Herbert Twin Redwoods Trailcamps: 1.5 miles
Twin Redwoods Trailcamp—Alder Trailcamp: .5 miles
Alder Trailcamp—Trailhead: .5 miles

See trail specifications on page 205

The Skyline Trail

TO GET THERE... The trail can be entered from Skylonda, Wunderlich County Park, and Huddart County Park.

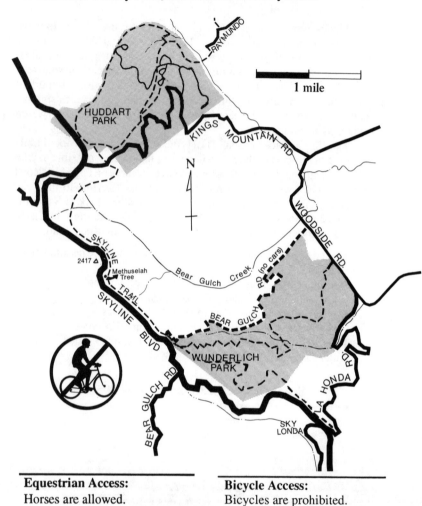

Equestrian Access:	Bicycle Access:
Horses are allowed.	Bicycles are prohibited.

Above the town of Woodside, the Skyline Trail parallels Skyline Boulevard for about 8.5 miles. The south end of the trail is at Skylonda, at the intersection of Skyline Boulevard and La Honda Road, and continues north through Wunderlich County Park, the California Water Company's Bear Gulch Watershed, and on through part of Huddart County Park .

The section from Wunderlich Park to Kings Mountain Road, near Huddart Park, is 4.7 miles. The trail crosses Kings Mountain Road .5 miles

The Methuselah Tree is 15 feet in diameter.

downhill from Skyline Boulevard. You can begin this walk at Wunderlich Park where the Bear Gulch Road forms the northern boundary of the park about 3 miles north of the La Honda/Skyline Boulevard intersection.

The Bear Gulch watershed is noteworthy for its trees. The largest of them is the "Methuselah" redwood, which is a short distance off the trail and just off Skyline Boulevard. It is 15 feet in diameter.

Several other old-growth redwoods also stand along the trail, though none are nearly that size. Exceptionally large Douglas fir trees are even more common, as are madrone and bay. In the northern part of this watershed, near Kings Mountain Road, you will find exceptionally large stands of rather rare golden chinquapin, often referred to as an oak, but actually more closely related to chestnut trees. It is easily identified by the golden-yellow underside of its leaves and by its sharp spiny nut hulls.

The Skyline Trail is well maintained and has little elevation range. Dogs and bicycles are prohibited. For more information, contact the San Mateo County Parks Department at (415)363 4020.

Soquel Demonstration State Forest

TO GET THERE. . . from Highway 17 take Summit Road and Highland Way east 9. 8 miles and turn right at a small bridge leading to a parking lot at the east end of the forest. The west entrance may be reached from Highway 17 by taking Summit Road east, head south 2.4 miles on Soquel San Jose Road, turn left on Stetson and right on Comstock Mill Road (1.4 miles from Soquel San Jose Road).

Soquel Demonstration State Forest was acquired by the California Department of Forestry in 1990 and is the first state forest to be added to the system since 1949.

A demonstration forest is a parcel of timberland used primarily for research, education, recreation, and the demonstration of innovative timber harvesting and forestry techniques.

This 3,000-acre forest is not a park, but it is open to the public, and is used by walkers and bicyclists to extend outings through The Forest of Nisene Marks State Park, which adjoins the property to the south. Horses are allowed in this property, but not in the adjacent state park.   At the headwaters of the east fork of Soquel Creek, including portions of Amaya Creek and Fern Gulch Creek, this area is covered mainly with second-growth redwood, and with some areas of oak, madrone, chaparral, and a few small groves of old-growth redwoods. The trails are old logging roads.

Pure stands of madrone grow along the Ridge Trail.

The picnic area makes a good outing destination. This wide, flat area between Soquel Creek Road and Soquel Creek displays a magnificent stand of big-leaf maple, mixed with oak, and a picnic table and sitting logs. November delivers a wonderful display of fall foliage as the maples turn bright shades of yellow and orange before shedding their leaves. Just across Soquel Creek Road is a cold, pure, calcium-carbonate spring that tumbles down the rocky slope, forming small stalagtite-like formations. Also nearby are a few old-growth redwoods.

The Sulphur Springs and Tractor Trails make steep ascents to the Ridge Trail, where you will find some pure stands of madrone and views

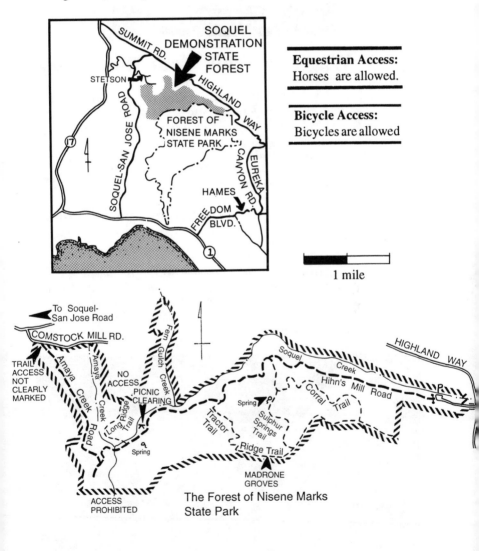

Equestrian Access:
Horses are allowed.

Bicycle Access:
Bicycles are allowed

1 mile

The Forest of Nisene Marks
State Park

into the Forest of Nisene Marks State Park.

The San Andreas Fault passes through this land, as evidenced by natural springs and sag ponds. In some areas are fissures formed by the October 17, 1989 Loma Prieta earthquake which was centered only 2 miles away in The Forest of Nisene Marks State Park.

This forest is particularly popular with mountain bikers and equestrians. Dogs are allowed on leash. It is open from dawn until dusk.

For more information, call the State Department of Forestry and Fire Protection at (408)475 8643.

SPECIAL SECTION

Where to Walk Your Dog

Dogs are not welcome on most trails in the Santa Cruz Mountains. Being natural predators they love to chase deer and rabbits; and even leashed canines can terrorize wildlife with their carnivore scent.

Policies concerning dogs.

Midpeninsula Regional Open Space Preserves: *Leashed dogs are allowed in designated portions of the following preserves.*

• Foothills Open Space Preserve.

• Fremont Older Open Space Preserve.

• Long Ridge Open Space Preserve, at the grassy area at the Grizzly Flat entrance.

• Windy Hill Open Space Preserve.

• Saint Joseph 's Hill Open Space Preserve.

Look for signs identifying where dog walking is allowed

State Parks: *Dogs are prohibited on park trails. They are allowed on leash at parking lots, campsites, and along paved roads. See the Pipeline Road in the Henry Cowell Redwoods State Park chapter.*

State Demonstration Forest: *Dogs are allowed on leash on all trails in the Soquel Demonstration State Forest.*

State Beaches: Dogs are not allowed on beaches from Gazos Creek to Ano Nuevo. Dogs on leashes are allowed north of Gazos Creek.

Santa Clara County Parks: Dogs are not allowed on trails, but may be taken on leash to road access parts of the following parks.
- *Almaden Quicksilver: Senator Mine area.*
- *. Lexington Reservoir.*
- *Mount Madonna: Valley View campground #1 and day use area.*
- *Sanbom-Skyline: Picnic areas.*
- *Santa Teresa: All road access sites except golf course.*
- *Stevens Creek: Picnic areas.*
- *Uvas Canyon.*

City Parks:
- *Arastradero Preserve: Dogs are permitted Monday through Friday only and must be leashed*

San Mateo County Parks: *Dogs are not permitted.*

Golden Gate National Recreation Area: *Dogs are allowed on leash.*

Stevens Creek County Park

TO GET THERE. . . from Highway 280 take Foothill Boulevard south. It becomes Stevens Canyon Road.

Stevens Creek begins in Monte Bello Open Space Preserve and tumbles down the steep east side of the Santa Cruz Mountains and on through Stevens Creek County Park.

This 777-acre park offers visitors a wide variety of activities, including picnicing, horseback riding, and archery. Boating and fishing are allowed in the Stevens Creek Reservoir.

Trails wander along tree-shaded streams and climb to scenic ridgetop vistas. You can explore the remnants of long-abandoned nineteenth century orchards and vineyards.

The climb to 1000-foot-high Lookout Point offers sweeping views of the Santa Clara Valley and nearby mountains. You can continue on into Fremont Older Open Space Preserve.

The 2-mile Stevens Creek Trail climbs through oak woodlands, and cuts through chaparral as it contours the steep slopes above the reservoir.

This is the oldest of the Santa Clara County parks, established in 1927. It has excellent family and group picnic areas. The park is open from 8:00 a.m. until half an hour after sunset. For more information call (408) 867-3654.

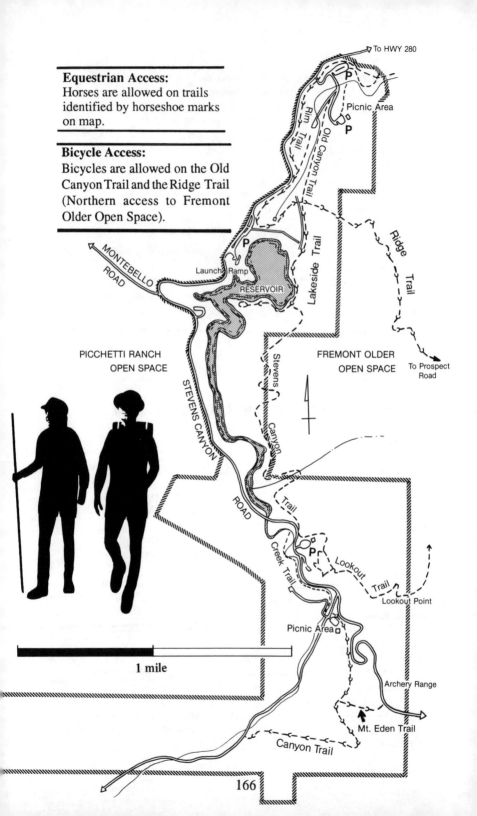

Equestrian Access:
Horses are allowed on trails identified by horseshoe marks on map.

Bicycle Access:
Bicycles are allowed on the Old Canyon Trail and the Ridge Trail (Northern access to Fremont Older Open Space).

To HWY 280

P

Picnic Area

P

Rim Trail

Old Canyon Trail

Ridge Trail

P

Launch Ramp

RESERVOIR

Lakeside Trail

MONTEBELLO ROAD

PICCHETTI RANCH OPEN SPACE

FREMONT OLDER OPEN SPACE

To Prospect Road

Stevens Canyon

STEVENS CANYON ROAD

Trail

P

Lookout Trail

Lookout Point

Creek Trail

Picnic Area

Archery Range

Mt. Eden Trail

Canyon Trail

1 mile

Teague Hill Open Space Preserve

TO GET THERE... it is just south of Huddart Park near Woodside. As of this writing there is no formed entrance.

This heavily-wooded preserve slopes eastward toward the town of Woodside. It is forested with madrone, bay, maple, oak, and scattered stands of second-growth redwood.

Being one of the newest open space preserves this area now has no official entrance or trail system.

Part of the Skyline Trail, which connects Huddart and Wunderlich parks, passes through part of the preserve.

For current information, call the Midpeninsula Regional Open Space District at (415) 691-1200.

Thornewood Open Space Preserve

TO GET THERE... from Highway 280 take Woodside Road (Highway 84) west and continue uphill on La Honda Road 1.5 miles from its intersection with Portola Road. From Skyline Boulevard take La Honda Road (Highway 84) east 1.9 miles. The preserve entrance is at a brick gate on the south side of the road.

An easy ramble through oak, chaparral and second-growth redwood will take you to a pleasant little pond called Schilling Lake. Here you are likely to enjoy the sounds of frogs and the sight of a mated pair of swans

This 148-acre former estate near Woodside was willed to the Sierra Club Foundation and was later given to the open space district. The impressive Thornewood mansion built in the 1920's is part of a 3.5-acre leased- out part of the preserve. Access to this area is by permit only. Bicycles are not allowed on the trail.

For more information, contact the Midpeninsula Regional Open Space District at (415)691-1200.

This is a steep canyon park, forested with canyon oak, black oak, coast live oak, tanbark oak, buckeye, madrone, bay, maple, and Douglas Fir. There are even a few introduced young giant sequoias on Table Mountain. The park is crossed by the San Andreas Fault, as evidenced by linear valleys and pressure ridges. At the trail intersection, a short walk down Charcoal Road, you will find one of the most easily seen Ohlone Indian grinding stones in the Santa Cruz Mountains.

This park is open from 8 a.m. until half an hour after sunset. For more information, call (408) 867-3654 or (408) 358-3741.

Equestrian Access:
Horses are allowed on the trail to Schilling Lake.

Bicycle Access:
Bicycles are allowed on the trail to Schilling Lake.

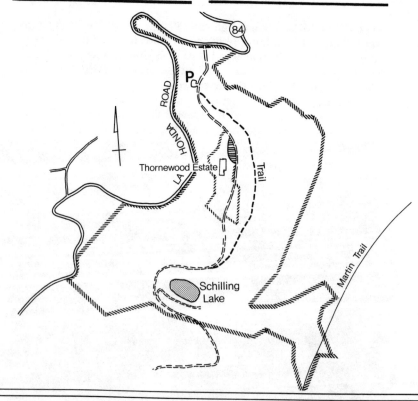

Half mile

University of California, Santa Cruz

**TO GET THERE... From Highway 1 in Santa Cruz take Bay Drive
north to the University Campus.**

The 8 colleges of this university are nestled in 2,000 gently sloped and
wooded acres of the Santa Cruz Mountains just above Santa Cruz.

An extensive dirt road, bikepath, and footpath trail system allows
students and visitors to explore the developed and undeveloped parts of the
campus. A good place to begin is at the north end of Heller Drive. From
here you can head north through second-growth redwoods, Douglas fir,
madrone, and chaparral. Motor vehicles and camping are prohibited.

You can also enter this undeveloped part of the campus on Empire
Grade Road 2.5 miles north of its intersection with Heller Road.

A gift of the Cowell family, this campus was once part of the Henry
Cowell Ranch.

For more information, call (408)459-0111.

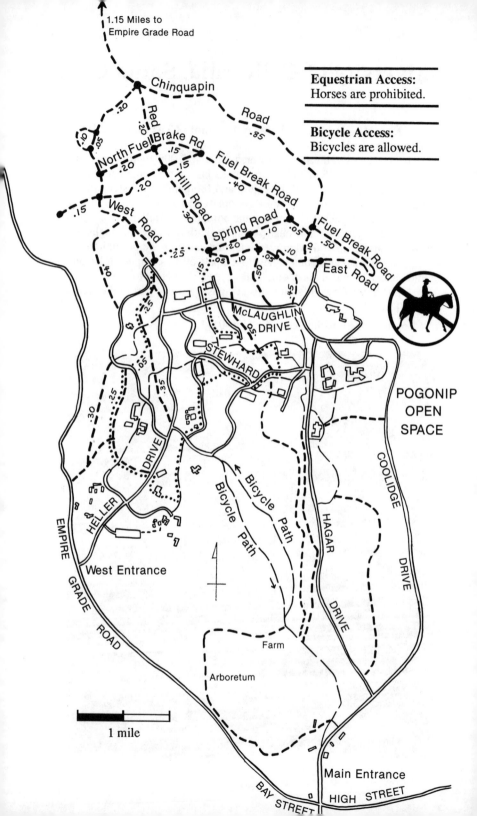

1.15 Miles to
Empire Grade Road

Chinquapin

Road

.85

.20

.20

Red

.20

.10

.65

North Fuel Brake Rd

.15

.15

.20

Hill Road

.40

Fuel Break Road

.20

.30

.15

West Road

Spring Road

.10

.05

Fuel Break Road

.40

.25

.20

.05

.10

.10

.50

.15

.05

.05

East Road

.25

.45

McLAUGHLIN
DRIVE

STEWHARD

.65

.35

POGONIP
OPEN
SPACE

.25

.30

HELLER

DRIVE

West Entrance

Bicycle Path

Bicycle Path

Bicycle Path

HAGAR

DRIVE

COOLIDGE

DRIVE

Farm

Arboretum

EMPIRE

GRADE

ROAD

1 mile

Main Entrance

BAY STREET

HIGH STREET

Equestrian Access:
Horses are prohibited.

Bicycle Access:
Bicycles are allowed.

Upper Stevens Creek County Park

TO GET THERE. . . the park is accessible along the east side of Skyline Boulevard north of Saratoga Gap. It can be reached via trail from Monte Bello and Saratoga Gap open space preserves.

There are so many open space preserves along this part of Skyline Boulevard that it is easy to overlook this 1,095-acre Santa Clara County park.

For many trail users this park is only known as a link along the Canyon Trail between Page Mill Road (See Monte Bello Open Space) and Saratoga Gap (See Saratoga Gap Open Space). However, there are another 4 miles of trails that are well worth exploring. Unfortunately, the Grizzly Flat and Table Mountain/Charcoal Road trails don't form a convenient loop trail. If you don't want to backtrack or walk 2 miles along Skyline Boulevard, consider adding 3.5 miles to your outing by including Long Ridge Open Space to your trip.

This is a steep canyon park, forested with canyon oak, black oak, coast live oak, tanbark oak, buckeye, madrone, bay, maple, and Douglas fir. There are even a few introduced young giant sequoias on Table Mountain. The park is crossed by the San Andreas Fault, as evidenced by linear valleys and pressure ridges. At the trail intersection, a short walk down Charcoal Road, you will find one of the most easily seen Ohlone Indian grinding stones in the Santa Cruz Mountains.

This park is open from 8 a.m. until half an hour after sunset. For more information, call (408) 867-3654 or (408) 358-3741.

Equestrian Access:	Bicycle Access:
Horses are allowed on all trails except the Alternate Trail.	Bicycles are allowed on all trail except the Alternate Trail.

SEE MAP ON PAGE 172

Uvas Canyon County Park

TO GET THERE. . . take Croy Road west from Uvas Road. It's west of Morgan Hill.

This 1,049-acre wooded park is tucked into a beautiful canyon west of Morgan Hill. Here you can escape the crowds and hike about 7 miles of trails along shady creeks and through wonderfully diverse forests of second-growth redwood, Douglas fir, bay, madrone, sycamore, bigleaf maple, buckeye, and several kinds of oak.

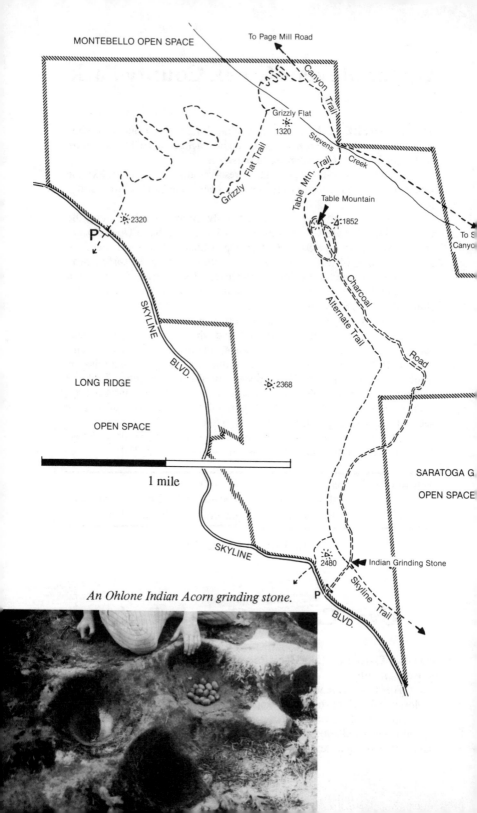

MONTEBELLO OPEN SPACE

To Page Mill Road

Canyon Trail

Grizzly Flat
1320

Stevens

Grizzly Flat Trail

Table Mtn. Trail

Creek

2320

P

Table Mountain

1852

To S
Canyo

SKYLINE

BLVD.

LONG RIDGE

OPEN SPACE

2368

Charcoal

Alternate Trail

Road

1 mile

SARATOGA G.

OPEN SPACE

SKYLINE

2480

Indian Grinding Stone

An Ohlone Indian Acorn grinding stone.

P

Skyline Trail

BLVD.

A great day hike can be taken on the loop trail beginning at the "nature trail" about a quarter mile beyond the bridge on the left side of the road. Follow the Swanson Creek Trail until it crosses Swanson Creek beyond the Old Hot House Site. This part of the route becomes the Contour Trail, which gains elevation and eventually intersects Alec Canyon Trail. Turn left here and return to the starting point. This loop is only about 3 easy miles and involves just a little uphill hiking. Short sidetrips from the loop trail can be made to Black Rock Falls and Basin Falls. Late winter and early spring is the best time to enjoy the waterfalls, which dry up in summer.

To make this route longer turn right on Alec Canyon Trail to explore the deep and shady second-growth redwoods along Alec Creek.

For an even more vigorous walk, climb Nibbs Knob by way of the Nibbs Knob Fire Trail, which gains about 1800 feet in less than 2 miles. Exposed to the sun, this is a tough hike on hot summer days. Take plenty of water. Great views of Loma Prieta, the Santa Clara Valley, and the Diablo Range will reward your efforts.

The waterfalls in this park are best enjoyed in winter and early spring.

You can continue on Nibbs Knob Trail to Summit Road and on south to Mount Madonna County Park.

The park has a family campground, available on a first-come, first-serve basis, and picnic facilities. For more information, call (408) 779-9232.

Equestrian Access:	**Bicycle Access:**
Horses are prohibited.	Bicycles are prohibited.

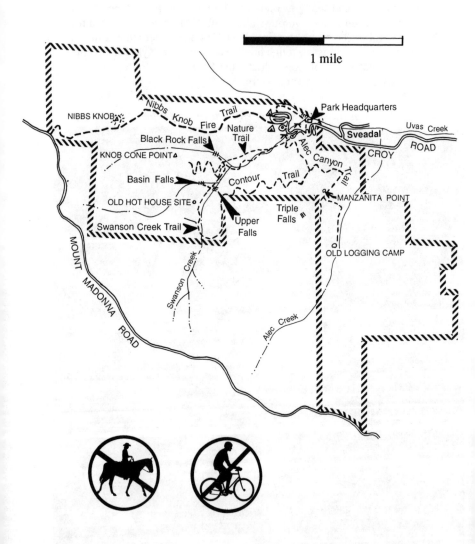

Villa Montalvo

TO GET THERE... take Saratoga-Los Gatos Road south of Highway 9 in Saratoga and turn southwest on Montalvo Road.

Villa Montalvo is a 175 acre cultural center, arboretum, and wildlife refuge in the hills west of Saratoga. The mansion is maintained by the Montalvo Association, and the remainder of the grounds have been under Santa Clara County jurisdiction since 1960.

Villa Montalvo is a very unique park. Because it is more of an educational than a recreational facility, there are no picnicking or camping facilities available. An easy 1.5 mile self-guided nature loop climbs about 400 feet into the Santa Cruz Mountains foothills. The park has only about 3 miles of trails, making it a good place for casual hikes and an excellent place to study the ecology of the east side of the Santa Cruz Mountains.

You can tell a lot about an area by the relationship between grasslands and oak trees. Oaks don't die out during the summer dry spell as do the annual grasses, and though they have deeper roots than the grasses, they need a lot more moisture to survive. A dense stand of oaks is an indication of available ground water, while a wide spacing of trees tells us that underground water is scarce and must be conserved among trees.

The arboretum is open to the public from 1 a.m. to 5 p.m. and the mansion is open from 1 p.m. to 4 p.m. The grounds and mansion were bought by California Senator and San Francisco Mayor James Phelan in 1911. Rooms on the estate are now rented to promising artists.

For more information, call (408) 867-0190.

Wilder Ranch State Park

TO GET THERE. . . it's just west of Santa Cruz, continuing along both sides of Highway 1 for about 3½ miles.

From the wild and rugged coast this 3,900 -acre park sweeps gently upward through grasslands and oakwoods and steep valleys filled with redwood and Douglas fir. An excellent trail system, totaling 28 miles, is open to walkers, mountain bicyclists, and horseback riders.

The best place to begin your visit is at the historic Wilder Ranch Cultural Preserve complex. Here you will find visitor information and see historic buildings and antique farming methods.

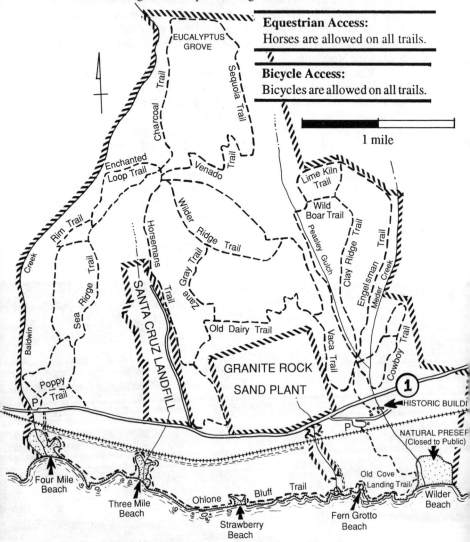

Equestrian Access:
Horses are allowed on all trails.

Bicycle Access:
Bicycles are allowed on all trails.

1 mile

Antique agricultural methods are sometimes demonstrated at Wilder Ranch. The 1891 horse barn is in the background.

The fern grotto, a beach cave with ferns growing from the ceiling, is one of many beautiful sights along the Ohlone Bluff Trail.

This land was once the Wilder Ranch, a prosperous dairy operation headquartered in a cluster of 1 9th-century buildings just off Highway 1. The oldest of these structures is an 1830's adobe built when this was Rancho Refugio, a Mexican land grant. A workshop with water-powered machinery, a dairy barn built of hand-hewn timbers held together with wooden pegs, a horse barn, 2 houses, and several other historic buildings remain from the period before 1900. These buildings are in the process of being restored for use as a park interpretive center and agricultural history exhibit.

After nearly a century of family ownership, the Wilders sold the ranch in the late 1960's to a development company which intended to convert the land to housing and commercial facilities. But when public opposition doomed this plan the state purchased the property in 1975, though it is only now starting to become publicly accessible.

Several areas will continue to have restricted public access, including a beach used for nesting snowy plovers, the marsh at the mouth of Meder Creek, and about 600 acres of farmland that will be kept in brussells sprouts.

A beautiful natural beach grotto carpeted with ferns is one of the main attractions along the coast.

As you travel into the backcountry of this park you will climb through a progression of nearly level areas followed by steep rises,

---

MARINE TERRACES

Fault movement has rapidly uplifted the Santa Cruz Mountains, leaving step-like formations of marine terraces well above the high tide line. Formed by wave erosion, these terraces are particularly noticeable along the coast between Half Moon Bay and Santa Cruz.

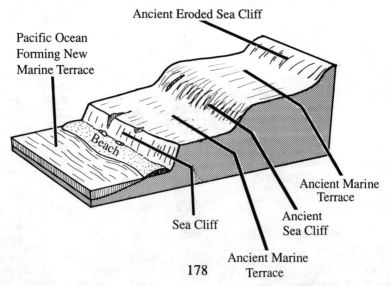

Ancient Eroded Sea Cliff

Pacific Ocean
Forming New
Marine Terrace

Beach

Sea Cliff

Ancient Marine Terrace

Ancient Sea Cliff

Ancient Marine Terrace

178

creating a step like effect. The flat areas are ancient marine terraces, formed by the erosion of ocean waves, and the steep areas between the terraces are ancient sea cliffs. The continuing uplift of the landscape by earthquakes and the incessant erosion of the waves has created what may be one of the clearest examples of marine terrace formations in the world.

For more information, call (408)426- 0505.

Windy Hill Open Space Preserve

TO GET THERE... take Skyline Boulevard 5 miles north of the Page Mill intersection and 2.3 miles south of the Woodside Road intersection. Park at the picnic area on the east side of Skyline. To reach the east (downhill) entrance to the preserve from Highway 280 take Alpine Road or Sand Hill Road west to Portola Road. The trailhead begins just north of The Sequoias on Portola Road.

If ever a hill lived up to its name, this is it. In fact, this preserve includes an area of high, grassy hills, seen from much of the Bay Area and exposed to the currents of wind that wash in from the coast. The preserve has about 14 miles of trails.

The Spring Ridge and Hamms Gulch trails can be combined to form a strenuous loop of 9 miles and an elevation range of 1,200 feet.

Take the Anniversary Trail from the picnic table area to the slope of Windy Hill itself and make a hardy ascent to the top. Here you will find one of the Santa Cruz Mountains' great views, with the bay and its cities spread out below. This windswept point is perfect for kite flying, with no entangling trees or telephone wires.

The grove of Monterey cypress just below Windy Hill to the east was planted as a wind break bordering the old Orton ranchhouse.

The southern part of the preserve is largely covered with chaparral, and madrone, bay, and Douglas fir woodlands. To explore this area, walk or drive just under a mile from the picnic area to the gate at the dirt road

Equestrian Access:
Horses are allowed on all trails except the Anniversary Trail.

Bicycle Access:
Bicycles are prohibited on Anniversary Trail, Eagle Trail, Hamms Gulch Trail, Razorback Ridge Trail, and Lost Trail.

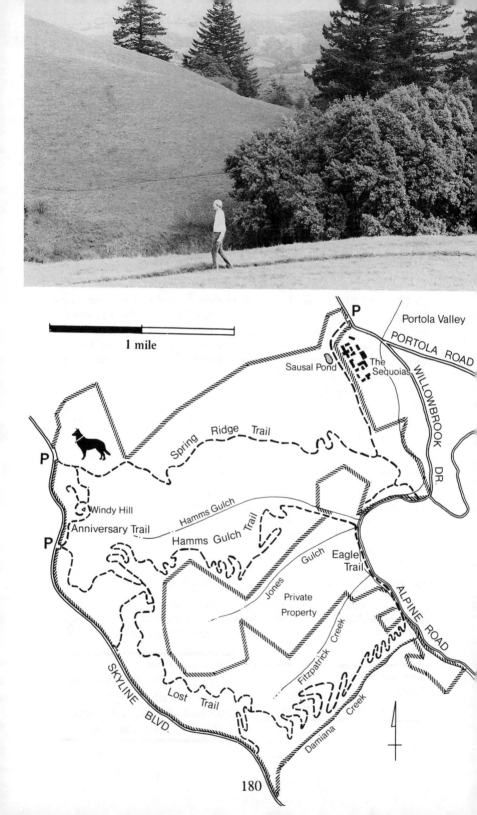

P

Portola Valley

PORTOLA ROAD

WILLOWBROOK DR.

Sausal Pond

The Sequoias

1 mile

Spring Ridge Trail

P

Windy Hill

Anniversary Trail

Hamms Gulch

Hamms Gulch Trail

P

Jones Gulch

Eagle Trail

Private Property

ALPINE ROAD

Fitzpatrick Creek

SKYLINE BLVD.

Lost Trail

Damiana Creek

that intersects Skyline. Either walk on the maintained dirt road, or turn south just beyond the gate on the deteriorated old ranch roads.

The western slopes of Windy Hill have been designated for use by non-motorized model gliders by permit only.

The Spring Ridge Trail connects Skyline Boulevard with Portola Road and Portola Valley 3.5 miles and 1260 feet below. Near the bottom of the trail, next to The Sequoias, is Sausal Pond.

Dogs on leash are allowed in designated areas.

For more information about this 1,132-acre preserve call the Midpeninsula Regional Open Space District at (415)691-1200.

Wunderlich County Park

TO GET THERE... take Woodside Road west from Interstate 280. Turn in at the parking lot at 4040 Woodside Road, about 2 miles southwest of the town of Woodside.

This is one of the most ecologically diverse and scenically beautiful parks east of Skyline Boulevard. Its 942 acres are especially popular with equestrians from nearby Woodside.

From the park entrance parking lot, at the Folger Ranch buildings, this looks like an oakwood-brushland park. But a short saunter up the hillside reveals dark, cool groves of second-growth redwoods, open grassy meadows, and nearly pure stands of Douglas fir. This is a steep park, with an elevation range of more than 1,650 feet; but it has excellent trails that are graded to avoid excessively strenuous climbs.

A beautiful half day, 4.75 mile excursion can be enjoyed by combining the Bear Gulch and Alambique trails. From the parking lot hike uphill on Bear Gulch Trail, passing through live oak groves and pockets of redwoods in shady creek beds.

Along the trail stands the rotting remains of a fence built when Simon Jones owned the property in the latter part of the nineteenth century. You will also find a long trough running up the hill. This is one of several skid trails created by oxen dragging redwood logs down the mountain between about 1850 and 1865 to provide lumber for Bay Area cities. The forest has re-grown, but this furrow will probably remain for centuries. You will also see large Douglas fir trees with low sprawling branches, indicating that at one time these trees were in open meadowland which was overgrown with trees when cattle grazing ceased.

Suddenly the forests give way to a beautiful meadow, covered with native bunch grasses and introduced perennials. There are sweeping views that make this a great place to stop and relax for awhile.

See trail specifications on page 205

1 mile

SKYLINE BLVD

Skyline Trail

Alambique Trail

Alambique Creek

Bear Gulch

Oak Trail

Meadow Trail

Giant Redwood

Madrone Trail

Redwood Trail

Trail

Trail

Trail

Alambique Trail

Loop Trail

Trail

P

ENTRANCE

HONDA RD

WOODSIDE ROAD

182

The Alambique Trail heads downhill, through all the park's native plant communities, and passing such introduced species as Monterey cyprus, eucalyptus, and olive trees. Be sure to pause and admire the enormous first-growth redwood on the north side of the trail—the kind you wouldn't expect to see east of Skyline. You will also see the ruins of old ninteenth century wagon bridges along the way.

If you have a few hours take the 5- mile round trip from the meadows to Skyline and back. From Bear Gulch Trail, head uphill on Alambique Trail to the top of the ridge and then gambol down the Skyline Trail and back to Alambique Creek, which flows along the course of a branch of Pilarcitos Fault. Notice that the rock suddenly changes from sandstone to shale as you cross the fault. Also notice that Douglas fir increasingly forests the steep hillside as you climb towards the Skyline ridge.

The Skyline Trail heads nortward, out of the park for 4.7 miles to Huddart County Park and Kings Mountain Road. See the Skyline Trail chapter for details.

At Salamander Flat a small reservoir once used for agricultural water storage is now a popular hangout for newts. Logged extensively to build San Francisco in the 1850's, the property was bought in 1902 by James Folger II, who built the house and stable.

This park is open for day use only. For more information, call the San Mateo County Parks Department at (415)363-4021.

Equestrian Access:	**Bicycle Access:**
Horses are allowed on all trails.	Bicycles are prohibited.

183

SPECIAL SECTION

Coastal Access Guide

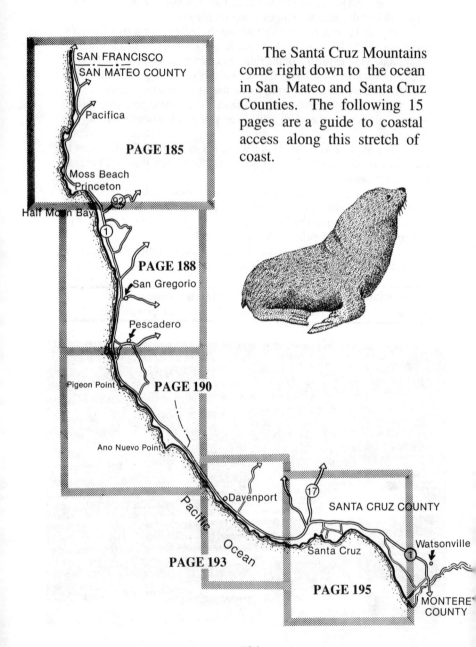

The Santa Cruz Mountains come right down to the ocean in San Mateo and Santa Cruz Counties. The following 15 pages are a guide to coastal access along this stretch of coast.

SAN FRANCISCO
SAN MATEO COUNTY

Pacifica

PAGE 185

Moss Beach
Princeton

Half Moon Bay

PAGE 188

San Gregorio

Pescadero

Pigeon Point   **PAGE 190**

Ano Nuevo Point

Pacific Ocean

Davenport

SANTA CRUZ COUNTY

Watsonville

Santa Cruz

PAGE 193

PAGE 195

MONTEREY COUNTY

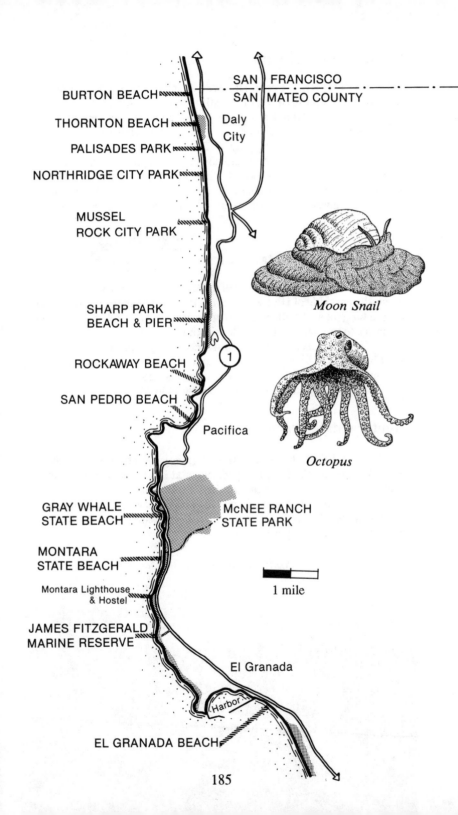

SAN FRANCISCO

SAN MATEO COUNTY

BURTON BEACH

THORNTON BEACH

PALISADES PARK

NORTHRIDGE CITY PARK

Daly City

MUSSEL ROCK CITY PARK

Moon Snail

SHARP PARK BEACH & PIER

1

ROCKAWAY BEACH

SAN PEDRO BEACH

Pacifica

Octopus

GRAY WHALE STATE BEACH

McNEE RANCH STATE PARK

MONTARA STATE BEACH

1 mile

Montara Lighthouse & Hostel

JAMES FITZGERALD MARINE RESERVE

El Granada

Harbor

EL GRANADA BEACH

Mussel Rock City Park

TO GET THERE... From Highway 1 in Pacifica take Palmetto Avenue north and turn left on Westline to the parking lot.

From the parking lot area you will enjoy awesome views up and down the coast. Be sure to bring your binoculars to view seabirds on the offshore rocks and migrating gray whales in winter.

Take the walkway northward downhill and climb over the concrete blocks to the beach. On your way down, to your right, you will see a large area where it appears the land has collapsed. This is the result of movement on the San Andreas Fault, and you are very near where it goes out to sea.

Gray Whale Cove State Beach

TO GET THERE... It's just south of Devil's Slide. From the parking lot on the east side of Highway 1, cross the road near the north end of the parking lot and walk a narrow road downhill to a 150 step wooden stairway to the beach. It's 5 miles south of Pacifica.

This small, beautiful crescent-shaped sandy beach is tucked out of sight by steep cliffs and bracketed by granite outcrops. Though this is a clothing optional beach, the weather is often not conducive to nudity.

For more information, call (415)728-5336.

Montara State Beach

TO GET THERE... It's just west of Highway 1 south of Devil's Slide and 7.7 miles north of Highway 92. Park at the Chart House restaurant or at a small dirt parking lot half a mile north.

Half a mile of golden orange sand make this a popular beach with volleyball players, sandcastle builders, and surfcasters. Just south of the beach are sea caves exposed at minus tide.

Volleyball on Montara Beach.

Montara Lighthouse Hostel

T0 GET THERE... It's on Highway 1 about 7 miles north of Highway 92 and .7 miles south of the Chart House restaurant.

You can spend a night in a dramatic coastal hostel setting adjacent to the old Montara lighthouse. There are 30 beds plus a kitchen in an old victorian house near the lighthouse. The hostel is closed from 9:30 a.m. to 4:30 p.. It is 25 bicycle miles from San Francisco's Fort Mason hostel.

For more information, call (415)728-7177.

James Fitzgerald Marine Reserve

T0 GET THERE... Take Highway 1 to the town of Moss Beach and turn west on California Avenue. It's about 10 miles south of Pacifica and 6.3 miles north of Highway 92.

A large rocky reef exposed at low tide makes this 3-mile long beach one of the best places in California to enjoy the amazing diversity of marine life. Get a tide table from a bait shop or sporting goods store and head for this reserve when the tide is low. Tidepool walks are conducted at low tide by rangers or docents. Special group tours can also be arranged.

Remember that it is illegal to remove or disturb marine life.

There is a hiking trail along the bluffs to the south of the parking lot, and there are picnic tables and a restroom amid the cypress grove near the parking lot.

The Seal Cove earthquake fault can be seen in the cliff about 100 feet north of San Vicente Creek.

For more information, call (415)728-3584 or (415)573-2595.

Fitzgerald Marine Preserve.

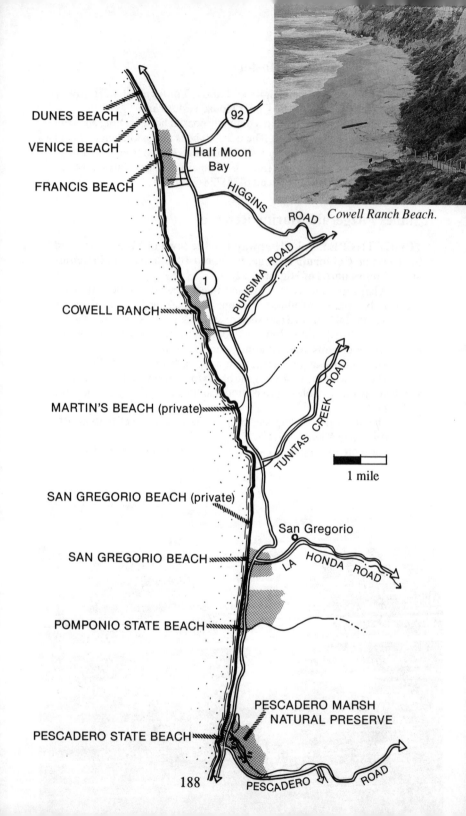

DUNES BEACH

VENICE BEACH

FRANCIS BEACH

Cowell Ranch Beach.

92

Half Moon
Bay

HIGGINS

ROAD

PURISIMA ROAD

1

COWELL RANCH

MARTIN'S BEACH (private)

TUNITAS CREEK ROAD

1 mile

SAN GREGORIO BEACH (private)

San Gregorio

SAN GREGORIO BEACH

LA HONDA ROAD

POMPONIO STATE BEACH

PESCADERO MARSH
NATURAL PRESERVE

PESCADERO STATE BEACH

188

PESCADERO ROAD

Cowell Ranch State Beach

TO GET THERE... The parking lot is just west of Highway 1 about 900 feet south of Half Moon Bay city limits and 3 miles south of Highway 92.

Most of this 1,300-acre ranch will be kept in agriculture. From the parking lot a half-mile dirt road trail takes you to a viewpoint overlooking the sea cliffs. A stairway trail descends to a beautiful secluded beach. There is no access to the next beach south where harbor seals breed.

Martin's Beach

TO GET THERE... Take Highway 1 about 7 miles south from Highway 92 in Half Moon Bay.

A fee is charged to drive the private-access toll road west from Highway 1 to a small seaside community and private beach. Impressive rock outcroppings and sandy beaches make this a pleasant area for beach relaxation and exploration.

There are some sea caves accessible at low tide. The rocky islands offshore are popular rest stops for harbor seals. Pups are born from late May through July. Surf fishing and surf netting are also popular.

San Gregorio Private Beach

TO GET THERE... From Highway 1 it's at the end of a paved toll road about 1.5 miles north of San Gregorio State Beach.

There is an admission fee to visit this clothing optional beach. It is open most weekends.

San Gregorio State Beach

TO GET THERE... It's at the mouth of San Gregorio Creek about 11 miles south of Half Moon Bay.

This beach has a large paved parking lot, a restroom, and picnic facilities. There is a small lagoon, good for wading in summer, formed on the broad sandy beach by San Gregorio Creek. There is a freshwater marsh east of Highway 1. The Portola expedition camped here in 1769.

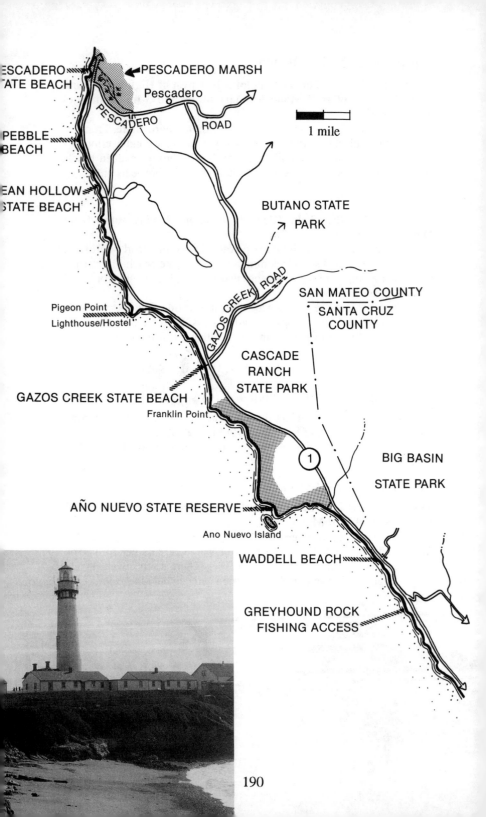

PESCADERO **←** PESCADERO MARSH
STATE BEACH

Pescadero

PESCADERO ROAD

1 mile

PEBBLE
BEACH

EAN HOLLOW
STATE BEACH

BUTANO STATE
PARK

Pigeon Point
Lighthouse/Hostel

GAZOS CREEK ROAD

SAN MATEO COUNTY

SANTA CRUZ
COUNTY

CASCADE
RANCH
STATE PARK

GAZOS CREEK STATE BEACH

Franklin Point

①

BIG BASIN

STATE PARK

AÑO NUEVO STATE RESERVE

Ano Nuevo Island

WADDELL BEACH

GREYHOUND ROCK
FISHING ACCESS

190

Pomponio State Beach

TO GET THERE... This beach is about 13 miles south of Half Moon Bay.

With paved parking, picnic facilities, and restrooms, this beach is ready for lots of visitors. Steep coastal bluffs overlook this long straight beach, which was named for an Ohlone Indian outlaw who fled mission life and became a bandit during the Spanish colonial period.

Pescadero State Beach

TO GET THERE... It stretches for about a mile along the coast near the intersection of Highway 1 and Pescadero Road.

Sand dunes, a wide beach, tidepools, and the mouth of pescadero Creek are a few of the attractions of this popular beach. Steelhead spawn up Pescadero Creek during the rainy season. It's just across Highway 1 from Pescadero Marsh.

Pebble Beach

TO GET THERE... It's just west of Highway 1 about 1 mile north of Bean Hollow Beach and 16 miles south of Half Moon Bay.

This small cove beach is covered with wave-smoothed agate, carnelian, quarts, serpentine, and other beautiful pebbles formed from an offshore quartz reef. There are good tidepools at low tide.

Bean Hollow State Beach

TO GET THERE... It's just west of Highway 1 about a mile south of Pebble Beach.

This small and intimate beach has a paved parking lot, picnic tables, and a restroom. There are good tidepools at low tide.

Pigeon Point

TO GET THERE... Look for a tall structure just west of Highway 1 between Pescadero Road and Ano Nuevo State Reserve.

You can't miss Pigeon Point. It's marked by one of the most picturesque lighthouses on the west coast. No other west coast lighthouse is taller, and only one other is as tall. This classic structure, built in 1872, will guide you to a rocky stretch of coast that is popular for tidepooling, surf fishing, and scuba diving.

You can stay the night here at the inexpensive and comfortable Pigeon Point Lighthouse Hostel, which is located in a series of cottages adjacent to the historic light. There are 40 beds, most in dormitory rooms, and private accommodations for families are also available. Daily check-in hours are 4:30 p.m. to 9:30 p.m. Reservations are recommended by calling (415)879-0633.

Gazos Creek State Beach

TO GET THERE... Look for the turnoff to the parking lot just west of Highway 1 near its intersection with Gazos Creek Road.

This is a good starting point for people who like long saunters along a remote wild seashore. Franklin Point, in Ano Nuevo State Reserve, is a short walk to the south. Wild salmon and steelhead spawn up Gazos Creek during the rainy season.

Ano Nuevo State Reserve
SEE PAGE 16

Waddell Beach

TO GET THERE... Adjacent to the Highway 1 entrance to Big Basin Redwoods State Park, this beach is just south of the high coastal cliffs that form the boundary with San Mateo County.

The most northerly beach in Santa Cruz County is located where Waddell Creek flows out to sea. This sandy beach is popular for windsurfing and the coastal bluffs are sometimes used for hang gliding.

Red, White, and Blue Beach

T0 GET THERE... Take Highway 1 north 7 miles from Santa Cruz or 4.2 miles south from Davenport and watch for a red, white, and blue mailbox. Take Scaroni Road toward the ocean.

This is a private clothing optional beach which is protected from wind by rocky headlands. An entrance fee is charged to use camping and picnicking facilities, restrooms, and showers. No dogs or cameras are allowed.

For more information, call (408)423 6332.

Davenport

Across from this town's shops and restaurants along Highway 1 is a parking lot where you can follow paths along the rim of a bluff overlooking the sea. This is a good place to see gray whales on their annual southbound winter migration. To the south a path descends to an inviting sandy beach bordered by impressive vertical cliffs. Even more impressive is a large man-made tunnel cut through solid rock where a creek now flows.

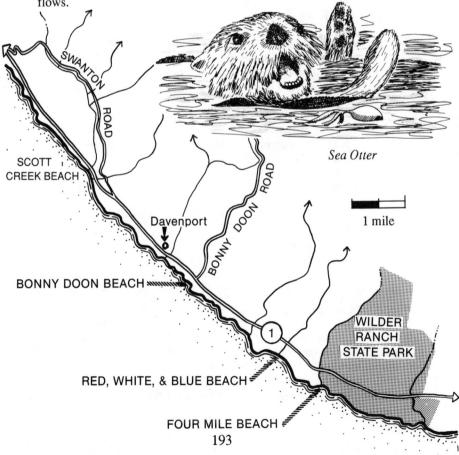

Sea Otter

1 mile

SWANTON ROAD

SCOTT CREEK BEACH

Davenport

BONNY DOON ROAD

BONNY DOON BEACH

1

WILDER RANCH STATE PARK

RED, WHITE, & BLUE BEACH

FOUR MILE BEACH

193

Greyhound Rock

T0 GET THERE... Look for the parking lot along Highway 1 about 19 miles north of Santa Cruz and 7 miles north from Davenport. It is 1.4 miles south of Waddell Beach.

A steep, paved trail leads down the rugged bluffs to a magnificent beach and rocky shore with rock outcroppings just offshore.

An outstanding place for rock fishing, surf netting, scuba diving, and beach combing, this is a California state fish and game reserve. There are picnic tables and a restroom on the bluff overlooking the beach. The reserve is open from 6 a.m. until 10 p.m.

Scott Creek Beach

TO GET THERE... It's at the mouth of Scott Creek, 3.6 miles south of Greyhound Rock.

This broad sandy beach is popular with hang gliders. It has an exceptional freshwater wetland just east of Highway 1.

Bonny Doon Beach

T0 GET THERE... About a mile south of Davenport, park at the intersection of Highway 1 and Bonny Doon Road. Cross the railroad tracks and continue down to the beach.

This is a beautiful and fairly small round shaped sandy beach nearly enclosed by rock outcroppings which protect it from wind. Clothing is optional.

194

Four Mile Beach

TO GET THERE... It's at the west side of Wilder Ranch State Park at the mouth of Baldwin Creek.

Take the dirt road from the west side of the railroad tracks downhill to a wide sandy beach. There is a large freshwater marsh at the beach.

Wilder Ranch State Park

SEE PAGE 176

Long Marine Laboratory

T0 GET THERE... From Highway 1 in Santa Cruz turn south (seaward) on Western, right on Mission, left on Natural Bridges Drive, then right on Delaware.

Anyone interested in marine biology will enjoy a free docent-led tour of this marine research facility operated by the University of California Center for Coastal Marine Studies. It has aquariums, marine mammals, and a blue whale skeleton. The laboratory is open daily except Monday from 1-4 p.m.

For more information call (408)429-2464.

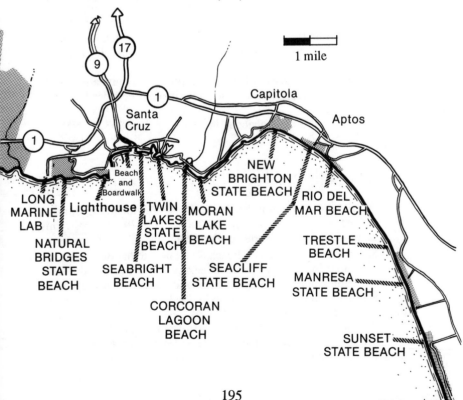

195

Natural Bridges State Beach

TO GET THERE... Take Highway 1 to near the west end of Santa Cruz, turn south on Swift Street , and turn right on West Cliff Drive.
This small park has many attractions, including a crescent-shaped beach, tidepools, good surfing, picnic sites, and of course the famous monarch butterfly overwintering grove. Despite its name, all but one of the natural stone arches at the beach have collapsed.

Monarch butterflies west of the Rocky Mountains, some from as far away as western Canada, migrate each fall to ancestral groves along the California coast to avoid freezing in the winter. They are first seen at Natural Bridges in October and most are gone by March. The Eucalyptus grove in the small canyon near the visitors center hosts one of the largest overwintering colonies in the state, greatly surpassing the more famous assemblage at Pacific Grove. The eucalyptus not only provide support for large clusters of butterflies and protection from ocean winds, but their winter blossoms provide a valuable food source. This grove is the only official Monarch Natural Preserve in California.

Because monarchs have a hard time flying when the temperature dips below 55 F, on cool days look for multitudes of the insects clustered together on branches hanging down under their weight. These clusters may be so motionless that at first you may not even recognize them as being composed of butterflies.

As the temperature rises, these inanimate butterfly clusters come to life and the air is filled with the amazing sight of countless orange and black creatures fluttering amid the eucalyptus. For this reason, calm and mild days are best for viewing.

In late January and early February, especially on mild afternoons, monarch males and females couple together mating. Females leave the grove soon after.

For more information about the park, call (408)323-4609. or (408)688-3241.

Santa Cruz City Beaches

At **Lighthouse Point** is the **Mark Abbott Memorial Lighthouse**, now operated as a surfing museum. Call (408)429-3429 for details. This is a great place to watch surfers. Sea lions hang out on an offshore rock.

Santa Cruz Beach, along Beach Street next to the Boardwalk, is the most popular and crowded beach in the city. Be sure to visit the half-mile long **Municipal Pier**. The beach has public restrooms and lifeguards.

Seabright Beach, between the Boardwalk and Santa Cruz Harbor along East Cliff Drive, has public restrooms and summer lifeguards. Call (408)688-3241 for more information. **Twin Lakes State Beach**, along East Cliff Drive just south of the Santa Cruz Harbor, covers 110 acres, including a lagoon behind the beach. For details call (408)688-3241.

196

Moran Lake Beach, near Lake Avenue, Sunny Cove Beach, at the end of Johans Beach Drive, and Lincoln Beach at the end of 14th Avenue, are all in residential areas and are less crowded than other beaches. They are along East Cliff Drive.

New Brighton State Beach

TO GET THERE... It's in Capitola just west of Highway 1, about 4 miles south of Santa Cruz.

This sandy beach, adjoining Seacliff Beach, has interpretive nature trails on the bluff, showers, firepits, and more than 100 well developed campsites amid a Monterey pine forest. Look for seashell fossils in the cliffs.

For more information, call (408)475-4850 or (408)688-3241.

Seacliff State Beach

TO GET THERE... In Aptos, it is off Highway 1 about 5 miles south of Santa Cruz.

This popular 85-acre beach stretches for about 2 miles along the coast. It is often crowded on warm days. There are 26 campsites available on a first-come, first-served basis, and a picnic area.

The fishing pier leads to a 435-foot long concrete ship, the Palo Alto, which was built during World War I. There was once a dance floor on the ship deck before the vessel broke up in a storm. No fishing license is needed when fishing from the public pier. This beach is at the northernmost range of the pismo clam.

For more information, call (408)688-3222 or (408)688-3241.

Manresa State Beach

T0 GET THERE... From Highway 1 take Mar Monte Avenue to San Andreas Road.

Take the long, steep, wooden stairway down to this beach from the parking lot. It is popular with pismo clam diggers from September through April, and with surfers and sunbathers. There are restrooms and outdoor showers.

For more information, call (408)688-3241 or (408)724-1266.

Sunset State Beach

T0 GET THERE... Take the Mar Monte exit from Highway 1 and head south on San Andreas Road. Then take Sunset Beach Road or Beach Road toward the ocean.

This 218-acre beach spreads across 7 miles of sandy beachfront. It has 90 campsites and picnic sites. Spring wildflowers are abundant on the bluffs. Usually foggier than Seacliff Beach, this beach is popular for surf fishing. Pismo clams are gathered from September until April.

The Palm Beach Unit, at the end of Beach Road, has a broad sandy beach backed by low dunes.

For more information, call (408)724-1266 or (408)688-3241.

Organizations & Agencies

Audubon Society: (Outings and conservation); Santa Clara valley Chapter: 22221 McClellan Rd., Cupertino, CA 95014; Sequoia Chapter: 30 W. 39th Ave., San Mateo, CA 94403; (415)345-3724.

Bay Area Mountain Watch: (Protection of San Bruno Mountain); P.O. Box AO, Brisbane, CA 94005.

California State Parks Department: (Santa Cruz Mountains Regional Office); Henry Cowell Redwoods State Park, Felton, CA 95018; (408) 688-3241.

Committee For Green Foothills: (Conservation); 3921 E. Bayshore Rd., Palo Alto, CA 94303; (415)962-9876.

Coyote Point Museum: (Environmental Education); Coyote Point, San Mateo, CA 94401; (415) 342-7755.

Environmental Volunteers: (Nature education for children): 3921 E. Bayshore Rd., Palo Alto, CA 94303; (415)961-0545.

Friends of Filoli: (Tours and special events at the Filoli estate); Canada Road, Woodside, CA 94062; (415) 364-2880.

Hidden Villa Association: (Environmental education and hostel); 26870 Moody Rd., Los Altos Hills, CA 94022; (415) 949-8660.

Midpeninsula Regional Open Space District: (Docent walks and open space information); 330 Distel Circle, Los Altos, CA 94022; (415)691-1200.

Monterey Bay Natural-Historical Association: (Wilder Ranch activities); c/o State Parks and Recreation Dept., 7500 Soquel Dr., Aptos, CA 95003.

Mountain View Parks Department: (Deer Hollow Farm); 201 S. Rengstorff Ave., Mountain Veiw, CA 94040; (415)903-6326 or (415)968-0364.

New Almaden Quicksilver County Park Association: (Historic and recreational activities); P.O. Box 124, New Almaden, CA 95042.

Peninsula Conservation Center: (Conservation activites and environmental library); 3921 E. Bayshore Rd., Palo Alto, CA 94303; (415) 494-9301 .

Peninsula Open Space Trust: (Acquisition and protection of open space); 3000 Sand Hill Rd., Menlo Park, CA 94025; (415) 854-7696.

Responsible Organized Mountain Pedalers (ROMP): (Off-road bicycle advocacy); P.O. Box 1723, Campbell, CA 95009-1723; (408)534-1130.

San Mateo County Parks Department: County Office Building, Redwood City, CA 94063; (415) 363-4020.

Santa Clara County Parks Department: 298 Garden Hill Dr., Los Gatos, CA 95030; (408) 358-3751.

The Santa Cruz Mountains Natural History Association: (Nature education); 101 North BigTrees Rd., Felton, CA 95018;(408) 335-3174

The Santa Cruz Mountains Trail Association: (Trail building and maintenance); P.O. Box 1141, Los Altos, CA 94022.

Sempervirens Fund: (Parkland acquisition); P.O. Box 1141, Los Altos, CA 94022; (415) 968-4509.

Sierra Club: (Outings and conservation); Loma Prieta Chapter: 3921 E. Bayshore Rd., Palo Alto, CA; (415)390-8494.

Trail Center: (Trail building, maintenance, and information); 4898 El Camino Real, Office 205A, Mountain View, CA 94022; (415) 968-7065.

Whole Access: (Handicapped access advocates); 517 Lincoln Avenue, Redwood City 94061

Youth Science Institute: (Wildernessinstruction and leadership development); 296 Garden Hill Drive, Los Gatos, CA 95030; (408) 356-4945.

SPECIAL SECTION

Peninsula Open Space Trust

Since 1977 Peninsula Open Space Trust (POST) has been instrumental in preserving more than 23,000 acres of threatened open space in Santa Clara and San Mateo Counties.

This private, nonprofit land trust works with national, state, county, and regional park and open space agencies to protect farmlands, beaches, forests, meadows, and baylands.

POST made the downpayment on the Phleger Estate, which is now part of the Golden Gate National Recreation Area. It purchased the Cowell Ranch just south of Half Moon Bay to maintain agricultural use and provide beach access. It helped prepare a 5-year restoration plan for Pescadero Marsh. The organization also acquired spectacular San Pedro Point in Pacifica and added land to Windy Hill Open Space Preserve.

To accomplish these and many other important achievements your help is needed by joining: Peninsula Open Space Trust at 3000 Sand Hill Road 4-135, Menlo Park, CA 94025; (415)854-7696.

Trail Specifications

	Maximum Grade of Trail	Average Grade of Trail	Minimum Trail Width	Average Trail Width	Trail Conditions
Almaden Quicksilver County Park					
Mine Hill Trail	20%	5%	10′	12′	Gravel, soil, some rocky
Randal Mine Trail	12%	1%	10′	12′	Graded
Guadalupe Trail	14%	3%	8′	10′	Graded
Hacienda Trail	30%	10%	8′	10′	Graded
Big Basin Redwoods State Park					
Skyline-to-the-Sea Trail: Park HQ to Berry Creek	18%	0–8%	30″	36″	Compacted Earth
Skyline-to-the-Sea Trail: Rancho Del Oso Section	10%	0–6%	48″	72″	Compacted Earth – Roadbed
Redwood Trail	6%	0–4%	48″	48″	Decomposed Granite

	Maximum Grade of Trail	Average Grade of Trail	Minimum Trail Width	Average Trail Width	Trail Conditions
Howard King Trail	15%	5–10%	36″	36″	Rutted, rocky
Pine Mtn. Trail	20%	8–15%	30″	36″	Rutted, steep, rocky
Lane Sunset Rim Trail	18%	6–8%	30″	36″	Compacted earth, rutted

Butano State Park

	Maximum Grade of Trail	Average Grade of Trail	Minimum Trail Width	Average Trail Width	Trail Conditions
Creek Trail	15%	5–12%	30″	36″	Compacted earth,
Doe Ridge Trail	20%	6–12%	30″	36″	Compacted earth, rocky
Goat Hill Trail	20%	8–15%	30″	36″	Compacted earth, steep
Olmo Fire Trail	20%	8–15%	4′	6′	Compacted earth, steep
Butano Fire Trail	20%	8–15%	30″	36″	Compacted earth, steep
Jackson Flats Trail	20%	8–15%	30″	36″	Compacted earth, steep rutted

Calero County Park

	Maximum Grade of Trail	Average Grade of Trail	Minimum Trail Width	Average Trail Width	Trail Conditions
Juan Crespi Trail	20%	3%	8′	10′	Compacted
Los Cerritos Trail	10%	2%	8′	10′	Compacted
Perra Trail	18%	10%	8′	10′	Compacted
Figueroa Trail	15%	2%	8′	10′	Compacted
Cherry Cove Trail	30%	1%	8′	10′	Compacted

Castle Rock State Park

	Maximum Grade of Trail	Average Grade of Trail	Minimum Trail Width	Average Trail Width	Trail Conditions
Ridge Trail	12%	6–13%	30″	36″	Compacted soil, rocky
Saratoga Gap Trail	12%	7–14%	30″	36″	Compacted soil, rocky
Castle Rock Whole Access Trail	6%	2–3%	48″	48″	Compacted decomposed granite

Edgewood County Park

	Maximum Grade of Trail	Average Grade of Trail	Minimum Trail Width	Average Trail Width	Trail Conditions
Serpentine Trail	10%	5%	18″	36″	Gravel, soil
Service Road	8%	4%	9′	9′	Gravel, soil
Sylvan Trail	10%	10%	18″	36″	Compacted soil
Ridgeview Trail	10%	5%	18″	36″	Compacted soil

	Maximum Grade of Trail	Average Grade of Trail	Minimum Trail Width	Average Trail Width	Trail Conditions

Forest of Nisene Marks State Park

	Maximum Grade of Trail	Average Grade of Trail	Minimum Trail Width	Average Trail Width	Trail Conditions
West Ridge Trail	20%	0–14%	30″	36″	Compacted soil, rutted
Aptos Creek Trail	15%	0–20%	30″	36″	Compacted soil
Prieta Grade Trail	12%	0–8%	32″	36″	Compacted soil
Aptos Creek Fire Road	10%	0–6%	48″	72″	Decomposed granite
Big Slide Trail	16%	8%	32″	36″	Compacted soil

Henry Cowell Redwoods State Park

	Maximum Grade of Trail	Average Grade of Trail	Minimum Trail Width	Average Trail Width	Trail Conditions
Ridge Trail	15%	5–8%	30″	36″	Compacted soil, sandy
Rincon Trail	15%	5–8%	30″	36″	Compacted soil, rocky
Graham Hill Trail	8%	0–8%	30″	36″	Sandy, rutted
Powder Mill Trail	20%	5–8%	30″	36″	Compacted soil
Redwood Trail	5%	0–3%	48″	48″	Decomposed granite
Pine Trail	15%	5–8%	30″	36″	Compacted soil, sandy
Eagle Creek Trail	20%	0–10%	30″	36″	Compacted soil, steps
Campfire Center Trail	2%	2%	48″	48″	Decomposed granite

Fall Creek Unit (Henry Cowell Redwoods)

	Maximum Grade of Trail	Average Grade of Trail	Minimum Trail Width	Average Trail Width	Trail Conditions
South Fork Trail	16%	5–15%	30″	36″	Rocky, ruttted, compacted soil
Cape Horn Trail	6%	0–4%	48″	6′	Road grade, compacted soil
North Fork Trail	10%	6%	24″	36″	Rocky, wet spots

Huddart County Park

	Maximum Grade of Trail	Average Grade of Trail	Minimum Trail Width	Average Trail Width	Trail Conditions
Richard's Road Trail	15%	10%	6′	6′	Gravel
Crystal Springs Trail	10%	8%	18″	36″	Compacted soil
Skyline Trail	18%	10%	24″	8′	Gravel
Chinquapin Trail	10%	5%	24″	36″	Compacted soil
Redwood Trail	15%	10%	18″	24″	Rutted

	Maximum Grade of Trail	Average Grade of Trail	Minimum Trail Width	Average Trail Width	Trail Conditions
Chaparral Trail	10%	5%	18″	36″	Compacted soil
Canyon Trail	10%	5%	18″	36″	Compacted soil
Dean Trail	10%	5%	18″	36″	Compacted soil

Mount Madonna County Park

	Maximum Grade of Trail	Average Grade of Trail	Minimum Trail Width	Average Trail Width	Trail Conditions
Merry-Go- Round Trail	8%		10′	14′	Compacted soil
Tanoak Trail	0%		4′	6′	Compacted soil
Ridge Trail	10%		14′	16′	Rocky
Bayview Trail	8-10%		4′	5′	Compacted soil
The Camp Trail	1-2%		4′	8′	Rutted, graded
Blackhawk Trail	14%		10′	12′	Compacted soil

Portola State Park

	Maximum Grade of Trail	Average Grade of Trail	Minimum Trail Width	Average Trail Width	Trail Conditions
Nature Trail	6%	6%	48″	48″	Compacted soil
Iverson Trail	18%	8-14%	30″	36″	Compacted soil
Summit Trail	20%	6-15%	30″	36″	Steep, compacted soil
Slate Creek Trail	15%	4-12%	30″	36″	Compacted soil
Peters Creek Grove Trail	18%	6-15%	20″	36″	Steep, narrow compacted soil

Sam McDonald County Park

	Maximum Grade of Trail	Average Grade of Trail	Minimum Trail Width	Average Trail Width	Trail Conditions
Towne Trail	10%	8%	18″	36″	Compacted soil
Ridge Trail	15%	10%	48″	10′	Gravel, soil

San Bruno Mountain County Park

	Maximum Grade of Trail	Average Grade of Trail	Minimum Trail Width	Average Trail Width	Trail Conditions
Summit Loop Trail	10%	8%	18″	36″	Rocky soil
Dairy Ravine Trail	10%	8%	18″	36″	Rocky soil
Ridge Trail	15%	8%	18″	8′	Gravel, soil
Eucalyptus Loop Trail	10%	8%	18″	36″	Compacted soil

San Francisco Fish and Game Refuge

	Maximum Grade of Trail	Average Grade of Trail	Minimum Trail Width	Average Trail Width	Trail Conditions
Sawyer Camp Trail	18%	4%	10′	10′	Paved
Crystal Springs Trail	15%	5%	18″	36″	Compacted soil

	Maximum Grade of Trail	Average Grade of Trail	Minimum Trail Width	Average Trail Width	Trail Conditions

San Pedro Valley County Park

Weiler Ranch Trail	5%	3%	8'	8'	Gravel
Valley View Trail	10%	8%	18"	36"	Compacted soil
Hazelnut Trail	10%	8%	18"	36"	Compacted soil
Big Canyon Trail	10%	8%	18"	18"	Compacted soil

Sanborn-Skyline County Park

Skyline Trail	7%	2%	2.5'	10'	Compacted soil
Sanborn Trail	20%	10%	2'	8'	Some ruts
Trail to Lake Ranch Reservoir	5%	0%	12'	16'	Compacted soil

Santa Teresa County Park

Ohlone Trail	15%	5%	2'	3'	Compacted
Hidden Springs Trail	20%	8%	8'	10'	Graded soil, shale
Ridge Trail	18%	8%	8'	10'	Graded, rocky
Peak Trail	20%	12%	8'	10'	Graded, rocky
Mine Trail	16%	6%	8'	10'	Graded, shale

Skyline-to-the-Sea Trail

Saratoga Gap to Big Basin		5-12%	24"	36"	Rutted, rocky in places, compacted soil
Big Basin HQ to BerryCreek	18%	0-8%	30"	36"	Compacted soil
Berry Creek to Highway 1	10%	0-6%	48"	6'	Compacted soil, roadbed

Wunderlich County Park

Skyline Trail	10%	5%	18"	36"	Compacted soil
Alambique Trail	10%	8%	48"	6'	Compacted soil
Bear Gulch Trail	10%	8%	18"	24"	Compacted soil
Madrone Trail	10%	5%	18"	36"	Compacted soil
Redwood Trail	10%	5%	18"	36"	Compacted soil

Wildlife Tracks

Most wild animals avoid people, but their tracks are often seen in muddy and dusty places. Here are some tracks you are likely to see in the Santa Cruz Mountains:

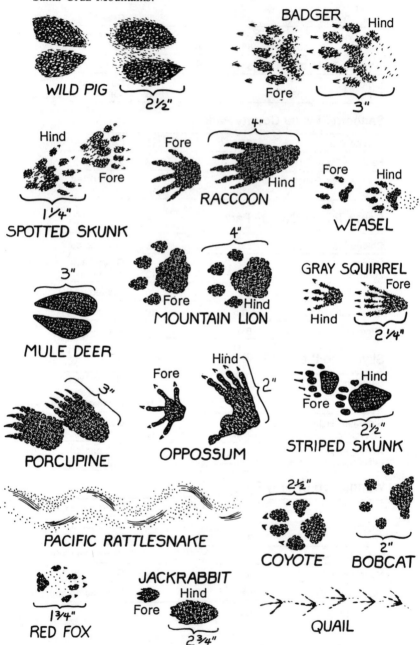

WILD PIG 2½"

BADGER Hind

Fore 3"

Hind Fore 1¼"
SPOTTED SKUNK

Fore 4" Hind
RACCOON

Fore Hind
WEASEL

3"
MULE DEER

4"
Fore Hind
MOUNTAIN LION

GRAY SQUIRREL Fore
Hind 2¼"

PORCUPINE 3"

Fore Hind 2"
OPOSSUM

Hind Fore 2½"
STRIPED SKUNK

PACIFIC RATTLESNAKE

2½"
COYOTE

2"
BOBCAT

1¾"
RED FOX

JACKRABBIT
Hind
Fore 2¾"

QUAIL

THE BAD NEWS:

GEOLOGISTS PREDICT THAT IN 10 MILLION YEARS THE SAN ANDREAS FAULT WILL MOVE LOS ANGELES NEXT TO THE BAY AREA

THE GOOD NEWS:

L.A. WILL KEEP MOVING NORTH AND EVENTUALLY DISAPPEAR INTO THE ALASKA TRENCH